ATHENS

BOOK TWO

BY

REA-SILVIA COSTIN, P.E.

ATHENS

Print ISBN: 978-1-0881-3907-3
Ebook ISBN: 978-1-0881-3916-5

Printed in the United States of America

Athens

Greece, Athens

I can't open that door yet.

I shut it closed, and I can't open it now.

Me, crying on the streets of Athens

Openly, in the middle of the day

The un mistaken feeling, that's where I belong.

How true it is

The saying,

That where you were born,

That's where you belong.

Athens in summer...

The beaches, my relatives there,

The freedom to walk on the streets,

The freedom to be alone,

The fullness and emptiness of being alone.

REA-SILVIA COSTIN, P.E.

I Dedicate This Book To
Athens-Greece, My Native Land

Athens

Table of Contents

Chapter 1: The Departure..3
Chapter 2: The Northern Train Station 9
Chapter 3: The Journey 12
Chapter 4: The Arrival 17
Chapter 5: Marula..19
Chapter 6: Nulli..24
Chapter 7: Licavitos 28
Chapter 8: The "Agapa"..31
Chapter 9: Odos Ermou 36
Chapter 10: The Beaches...39
Chapter 11: George..43
Chapter 12: George..46
Chapter 13: George-The Night Alone...............................50
Chapter 14: George-Good bye!..53
Chapter 15: Home Alone 56
Chapter 16: George-The Confrontation............................59
Chapter 17: Vangheli 63
Chapter 18: MARULA-The Confrontation.......................66
Chapter 19: The Telephones 70
Chapter 20: Vangheli...73
Chapter 21: Packing...76
Chapter 22: The Garsoniera 79
Chapter 23: The Safe Deposit Box 82
Chapter 24: Teresa..85

Chapter 25: Rania 87

Chapter 26: Maria 91

Chapter 27: The School 94

Chapter 28: Mimis 96

Chapter 29: Mr. Lavranos 100

Chapter 30: Costas 102

Chapter 31: Vasili..106

Chapter 32: Costas 109

Chapter 33: Evghenia 111

Chapter 34: The Workplace 114

Chapter 35: Costas 118

Chapter 36: Maria 121

Chapter 37: "The Epitropi" 124

Chapter 38: Alexander 127

Chapter 39: Mother 129

Chapter 40: Acropolis 131

Chapter 41: The Barzas Family...134

Chapter 42: Maria 138

Chapter 43: Maria 142

Chapter 44: The World Churches Services 144

Chapter 45: Dr. Barzas 147

Chapter 46: Vula 150

Chapter 47: Vuliagmeni 153

Chapter 48: Kiki 155

Chapter 49: The American Embassy 157

Chapter 50: Costas..163

Chapter 51: Raffia..165

Chapter 52: Raffia..167

Chapter 53: The show down..169

Chapter 54: Vuliagmeni 173

Chapter 55: The End 176

Chapter 56: Epilogue 1 178

Chapter 57: Epilogue 2 180

INTRODUCTION

"Athens" is the second book in a trilogy that spansthe life of three generations of strong women: the author's grandmother, Calliope, the author's mother, Thiana, and the author herself, Silver.

The first book "Thiana-AVDELA-A Macedonian Village in the northwestern Greece-Thiana's Native Land" —depicted the lives and events associated with Calliope's and Thiana's lives and Thiana's journey from her native AVDELA to Romania.

"Athens", the second book, depicts Silver's life while in Greece.

Silver, a young, inexperienced woman, fresh out of college, defects the Communist Regime in Romania, where she grew up, and goes back to her mother's native land, Greece, to make a life for herself and bring her family over from Romania.

One after an other, her dreams, fueled by her mother's stories, of finding acceptance, love, and security are crashed, as she is forced to face the harsh realities. After 14 months in Greece, Silver has to make the decision of her life: to come back to the Communist Romania or go further, alone, to America.

"Athens" is a love story, as the young heroine escapes from the restrictions of the Communist Romania, opens her self to love and freedom, and pays the high price that comes with both.

Silver is trying to fulfill the promise she made to her mother, Thiana, that she would go back to her native land, Greece, kneel down and kiss the ground. Through her tribulations, Silver found out that the past couldn't be recaptured, that her mother's dreams were only dreams, and she has to move forward with her life.

This is Silver's story and her coming to age.

Chapter 1

The Departure

It was summer of 1980 in Communist Romania, closed behind the Iron Curtain, cut off from the Western World. It had taken Silver and her mother years to obtain the passport for Silver to travel to her mother's native country, Greece. It had taken her mother several trips back and forth from Romania to Greece just to convince the Ceausescu Regime that the family had no intention of leaving Romania. Romania was Silver's father's native country.

Silver was in her twenties, rather tall, slender, her light brown hair cut fashionably short, like a thick brush around her perfect oval face. She was fresh from the University and Silver was embarking on the adventure of her life. Nothing from this point on would be the same. Nothing ever. The family's plan for her had been carefully crafted over the last months. She was going to visit her cousin in Greece and not come back. The family hung their hopes for the future on her. They were as one, pushing forward the family member with the best chance for achievement.

It was really Silver's mother's plan. She was the commander of their house. At least that was what her husband, Costin, fondly called her. He was a few years older than his wife was and he never challenged her authority or role in the house. Silver knew her father was the one who really made the decisions in his calm and good- natured ways. He merely gave his wife the impression she was in charge to make her feel important. Silver's mother, Thiana, was a pretty, middle-aged woman, small, and full of life and energy.

Silver had said her good-byes to her family and home in the seclusion of their big house, the night before leaving for the train station, After twenty years of fighting and struggling with unwanted renters installed by force by the communists into their home, the house was once again theirs. All of it. The front rooms and the back rooms, the bedrooms, the dining room and the hallways, the bathrooms. They just finished remodeling it. They painted each room a different color to match the antique ceramic stoves in the corners. And now that it was done, Silver had to leave.

Silver went from room-to-room trying to memorize all the details about the home where she grew up. God, she loved that house. They had all worked hard to fix it up. They had put so much love into it, as if restoring a work of art. They had stripped the old, dull layers of paint from the ceiling moldings and discovered the original gold paint. They'd waited twenty years to enjoy their house without the intrusion of strangers.

Would she ever see it again? Would she ever come back? She stepped into the dining room. Father was seated at the square oak table near the window, reading the newspaper. He wore the thick, green velvet housecoat they bought him for Christmas, even though it was summer. He had made a calendar for himself and was scratching off the days as they passed. His main pastime, these days, was to look out through the window and notice exactly what the neighbors were doing. Silver sat down on a chair opposite him so she could look into his beloved face and eyes. He looked so frail with the receding hairline and reading glasses, which made his eyes looking huge on his thin face. Would she see him again, ever? The pain, the anguish, and the indecision started to tug at her heart.

What was she about to do? Had she thought this out, carefully? Was it her decision to leave or, maybe, her mother's plan, her mother's desire to go back to Greece to be with her family? She caught herself short. She had to stop thinking like that, or she'd never make it out of the door. The decision was made for her; it was for the benefit of the entire family. She'd think about it later. Not now! She had to block it out of her mind for now and steel herself in order to be able to leave. God, she loved her father. He was so gentle, so calm. When everyone was losing his or her mind he remained calm and had a good word for everyone. She couldn't bear thinking of not seeing him again. Yet, he had agreed with Mother that she should leave. She wanted to leave too. Maybe there was hope for all of them. A better life. Freedom.

"Frangulitza, my sweet and smart little girl". He called her by the diminutive of her nickname. They called her Frantzi at home. The name stayed with her immediately after she was born and her father went to see her at the hospital. He barely hid his disappoint of not having a son, the second time around. Another girl and this one looked ugly. He'd glanced at her and said "God, she looks like Franz Joseph, the Austro-Hungarian Emperor. Look at her upturned nose." And her nickname remained Frantzi till this day. "I know we're going to succeed. You are like me, smart." he had said. He meant book smart, Silver thought. "Take care of yourself and when you can, bring the others to you. We're going to be all right here. Don't worry about leaving us behind. We have the house and we are all together. Take care of yourself. You'll be alone but remember we're always going to be behind you. A hundred percent, no matter what."

He was playing it cool, to encourage her. He was not going to show his emotions. As if nothing out of the ordinary was happening. She knew him better. There was a special bond between the two of them. They understood each other without words. They both shared a love for books and study; they both lived cocooned into their ivory tower of idealism. Had he said "bring the others to you?" He had not said "bring us to you." He did not include himself. Why?

Her mind was playing tricks on her. She would not dwell upon it any longer.

"I know that, father."

* * *

Radu, her brother, cornered her in their kitchen. "Do you really have to go?" he asked. His thick, dark blond hair fell into his big, brown eyes, which pleaded with her. Her "baby" brother, two years younger, was now bigger and taller than she was. He had developed into a handsome young man in his early twenties. He resembled their father so much.

They both stood by the old fashioned sink. The kitchen was done in blue, the walls and the ceiling included, and they had kept the old, squeaky hardwood floor. Silver could feel the air thick, heavy with unspoken emotions, tightly controlled. The pain, the fear, the unshed tears, the false, joyful façade.

"Yes. Mother thinks I should go to Greece and live with her relatives. Later, I'll bring all of you over there."

"I don't understand why you must. We're all right here. We have the house, we have jobs. Maybe we aren't going to be rich, or have the freedom to travel. Maybe we won't marry either, but at least we can be together."

"You know, we've talked about this many times. We all agreed I should go. Since I've a passport now, it's my opportunity."

"If you think you must, would you at least promise you'll take care of yourself? You won't become a prostitute or anything like that in order to survive?"

"Radu, I promise you. I'll do my very best to make something of myself. I'll never do anything you or I would be ashamed of."

His entire soul was showing through his eyes, his anguish, and the silent plea for her not to go, to stay together as the close-knit family they were. He needed her there. She had always been there for him. Now she felt as if she was deserting him.

*   *   *

In her bedroom, Silver said her farewell to her older sister, Magdalena. It was just recently that she had gotten her own bedroom separate from Mady, as the family called her. With her long black hair, hazel eyes and perfectly oval face, she resembled her father's sister Olga. They'd shared the same bedroom for twenty years. Recently, when the house had been emptied of renters, they restored it and Silver got her own bedroom. She painted it a soft rose color, matching the color of the ornate ceramic stove in the room. She bought new bedroom furniture with her first salary as an engineer.

"I'll miss you," Mady said in a small voice.

"I'll miss you too. We've done everything together for so long. I'll miss your practical advice. You always brought me back to reality when I tended to stray."

"Take good care of your self and when you can, bring all of us there. We'll be waiting for you."

"I know. And that's why I'm going."

No regrets from Mady. No second thoughts. She was an optimist. She was looking forward to what the future could bring them. All of them.

Mother joined them in the bedroom. She sat down next to them on the folding bed. It was not a comfortable bed but Silver liked the blue silk tapestry when she bought it. Silver could tell her mother was trying very hard to be courageous and cheerful. She looked over her mother's dear face. When had Mother's face become like that? All lined up, tense? Her eyes were swollen. Silver could tell she had been crying. Not in front of them, of course. Silver vowed to be as strong and not break down.

"Did you pack everything? Mother asked.

"I have the luggage ready. I'll wear your old dress for the trip. It'll bring less attention."

"That's good. Make sure you eat. I put some provisions for you in a handbag. Be careful in the train."

"I'll be careful."

"I called your cousin, Marula. She'll meet you at the train station in Athens. I told her to wait for you. Everything will be all right. My brothers will take care of you in Athens. Don't forget to call us the minute you arrive in Athens. I'll be waiting."

"Don't worry, I won't forget."

"Be careful what you say over the telephone. You know they listen to telephone conversations.

"I know, mother."

"You'll love Greece and Athens."

She hoped that was true. She had mixed feelings about her eminent departure. On one hand, her heart was heavy about leaving her family behind, well knowing that there would be repercussions from the Communist Government taken upon her family because of her departure. The separation itself, the thought that she might not see them again, was like a dark cloud hanging low upon her heart. But for herself, she was looking forward to seeing new places, meeting new people, and maybe falling in love. It was a great adventure waiting to unfold for her.

Chapter 2

The Northern Train Station

Silver, her mother, her sister, and her brother, loaded down with luggage, entered the Northern Train Station located in the heart of Bucharest. Tall and slim in her high-heeled sandals, wearing a simple dress, Silver led the way. At one o'clock in the afternoon, the train station swarmed with people. Trains left and arrived in the station from all directions in Romania. Bucharest was the central point of commuting, and was the capital of the country. The station was an old monumental style building. Flights of stairs led from the front and sides, with freight loading platforms on the opposite side of the building, assuring direct connections with buses and tramlines from all directions. Gray and doomed looking people waited in lines to buy tickets, hurried to catch trains, carried heavy suitcases, held small children tight in their arms, or dragged them by their hands. The fumes from the coal-fueled locomotives mingled with grease settled on the station's building and platforms. The reddish brown tile floor was darkened and slippery.

Silver and her family felt lost in the middle of the crowd. They didn't know which track her train was leaving from. Nobody paid any attention to them as they advanced between the train tracks on the covered platform. They looked as gray and doomed as everyone else did.

For the trip, Silver wore her mother's plum dress with long sleeves and high collar. Her long, slender neck and pale face and short light brown hair were set off by the dress's color. On her feet were sturdy, high-heeled sandals, the same plum color as her dress.

It was summer, the first of July, and a hot afternoon. Most people wore light, summer clothes. Because of her high heels, she was the tallest of their group. Father remained home. He had not come with them to the train station. Silver guessed it would have been too much for him.

They located the train that went to Bulgaria and passed through Turnu Severin, the frontier point in Romania, and from Bulgaria to Greece. It was an overnight trip to Athens, her final destination.

At the train station, the family play-acted for the benefit of the onlookers. As far as everyone could tell, Silver was only departing for a month's vacation in Greece, to visit with the cousins. No one else was there to say good-bye to Silver, not her colleagues and friends from her office, nor friends of the family, nor her cousins. Nobody knew about her departure. Not that Silver had any truly close friends. The friendships of her high school and college days were left behind, any romances long finished. Her colleagues from the office were distant; most of them had already married and had families. Even her cousins from her father's side of the family were already married. Silver did not feel particularly close to anyone, besides her family.

Finally, they found the train and the right compartment according to her ticket. Everyone helped Silver carry her luggage into the compartment and put it in the luggage nets. Her mother kissed her good-bye, and her sister and her brother did too.

"Make sure you call me the moment you arrive at Marula's," her mother said again. "Call collect."

The family left Silver alone in the compartment and went to stand outside on the platform besides the train.

Waiting for the train to depart, Silver leaned out the open window, trying to memorize everyone's faces. The train moved slowly out of the station. Silver stared at her brother, Radu, who remained on the platform. It might be the last time she would see any of them, despite all their best efforts.

No, she wouldn't entertain that thought, Silver decided. If she thought she wouldn't see them again, she wouldn't have the courage to go forward. To do what she had to do, she would have to block away any negative feelings, any regrets, any doubts she might have. She would have to think positively about the future and particularly the fact that her separation from her family was a temporary one.

Otherwise her feelings would overwhelm her and she would not be able to go forward. Inside, deep buried into her heart, she knew she was not prepared for life's hardships. She had lived until that moment cocooned in the love and care of her family. Her mother had taken care of the everyday miseries, dealing with the plumbers and the roofers and the unruly and pesky tenants. She had been shielded all her life from the harshness and spent most of her time studying and reading, her imagination aflame with the beautiful places she was going to visit and all the nonsense of the romantic novels she was practically feeding on daily. In the back of her mind, she knew she was still the small girl who refused to go the bakery on the corner of the street to buy a loaf of bread or who was too shy to ask a rude clerk for the correct change that she was owed.

Chapter 3

The Journey

The train was full of people. Hers was the third class passengers' car on an older train, with narrow compartments opening off the hallway. The compartments held up to eight persons, with two wooden benches facing each other. Silver sat next to the window. The train moved out of Bucharest's train station when four Russians officers came into her compartment and took the seats next to her. She watched with dread.

Her battered suitcases were jammed beneath the bench, and her packages thrown into the net above her seat, taking most of the luggage space in the compartment. Thankfully, the Russian officers didn't have much luggage, only briefcases, which they held tightly across their laps, and several Danubiana tires that they stashed in the corner next to the compartment's door. Romania was famous for its tire brand, Danubiana. When the officers came in, they had told the train conductor that they were going to Bulgaria.

Because the Russian officers were in the same compartment with her, perhaps the customs officers might overlook her. Certainly they would not search her luggage in front of the Russians. Thinking of the custom's point at Turnu Severin made Silver afraid.

If the customs officers were to open her luggage and see the things she was taking with her for her "short vacation," maybe she would be turned back at the frontier. The white fur hat would be hard to explain for a month's summer vacation in Greece. The same went for her embroidered sheep skin coat.

"Gavarite Paruski, Mademoiselle?" The young officer who addressed her was quite handsome in his impeccable dark blue uniform and white shirt.

"Da."

Silver brought her hand abruptly to her neck, checking the buttons of her high neck dress. Hopefully, nothing showed. Beneath her dreadful dress, at her neck and on her wrists, she wore all the jewelry she had received from her mother throughout the years. Her mother had brought the jewelry with her from Greece, beautifully handcrafted 18- karat gold bracelets.

Communist Romania's policy was that one could bring no gold or precious stones or artwork of any value out of the country. To try to do so could cause the person to go to prison. Horrid stories of people who were waiting years to get a visa to depart Romania had made their way back to her office in Bucharest. They were stripped of all their possessions, beginning with the houses they owned, which they had to sign over to the Government. Jewelry, art objects, everything was taken away from them.

After years of interrogations and endless forms filled out, just before they were allowed to leave the country, the customs' officers pulled even the gold capped teeth out of their mouths.

For a moment, Silver doubted she could remember the Russian language that she'd studied for eleven years in the elementary school and high school. Everybody was required to take Russian, starting from the second grade. In fifth grade one was allowed to pick up a second foreign language like French or English. Silver had studied French.

Silver never thought she'd use her Russian, but during the stress of the moment, trying to hide the true intent of her journey and gain their confidence, she remembered the forgotten language. The Russian officers were surprised that she spoke so well. The conversation with the Russians continued on smoothly. Silver was nice and polite on the outside, trying to play it cool, but inside she was like an overheated boiler ready to explode. She did not even have the courage to leave the compartment and go to the bathroom at the end of the hallway in fear that the Russians would take a peek at her luggage. Even though they didn't look the type to do so. They were polished and very civilized. But one never knew. Her mother's warnings were still sounding in her ears.

Time flew by and soon the train entered the frontier point at Turnu Severin. The train stopped, and the customs officers in gray uniforms entered the train to check everyone's identity and passports. If they had any doubts about a person, they opened their luggage and searched their belongings. Did she see some of the customs officers climbing the train with dogs kept tight on leashes? For the drugs, of course. She heard that they used specially trained dogs to smell the luggage for hidden drugs.

That was the moment Silver dreaded. She remained quiet in her corner. She tried to look very insignificant so that they would overlook her. She'd not say one word, or even look at them. The customs officers opened the door of their compartment, stopped in the doorway, and for a long frozen moment they looked around as if taking in every face, slowly sweeping their glances over them and all their belongings. What piercing glances. It was as if they were photographing every detail in the whole compartment. Then their demeanor shifted, and with smiling faces they saluted the Russian officers and easily started to converse with them in Russian. So they also knew Russian.

Silver wondered if the customs officers were tipped off before hand as to who was suspected of carrying drugs. When they had entered the compartment they had no dogs with them. Politely they asked to see the tickets and the passports, first of the Russian's and last of Silver's. They looked her over as if checking the picture on her passport against the real thing.

"We're going on vacation?" One of the custom officers asked Silver in fluent Romanian.

"Yes. No. I'm going to visit my relatives in Greece for a month." The answer came out of her mouth fast, like a straight arrow.

They, nodded their heads, saluted the Russian officers and left.

"Whoa! What a relief!" she thought. She could hear her own breath swishing loud out of her lungs. She had not realized that she had been holding her breath. Silver felt perspiration sliding down from her armpits along her underarms in little rivulets.

*　*　*

From that moment on, Silver knew she was free. Romania and the Ceausescu regime had been left behind. Unfortunately, so was her family, at least for now.

The train entered Bulgaria. The Russian officers left at Sofia. Silver relaxed.

Then she went to the car's restroom, located at the rear next to the exit stairs. The compartment was empty and she could stretch out on the bench and sleep. She unpacked the food her mother had prepared for her. Hard-boiled eggs and bread, snitzel and coffee. She ate at her leisure at the small retractable table in front of the window. The train was nearly empty.

The weather gradually changed as the train headed south. When Silver left Rumania it was merely warm, but moving south, the temperature became hot. Silver perspired in her long-sleeved dress. She felt secure enough to open her dress at the neck and roll her sleeves up.

The scenery outside the train's window also changed. The green leafy trees of Romania disappeared. Silver noticed the red clay soil, the yellow burned grass, and sparse smaller trees.

Chapter 4

The Arrival

The train entered Greece, and the air inside the compartment was stifling. Silver gazed at the landscape outside the window as the train traveled through Greece, her new home.

Her cousin, Marula, the daughter of her mother's older brother, Tacki, had invited her to stay with her family. Her mother had spoken with Marula. The plan was that once in Greece Silver was to request political asylum and remain there.

The scenery outside the train's window was gray. There wasn't much industrial development, factories, or smoke leaving chimneys, nor the towers for water storage Silver was accustomed to in Romania. Silver was afraid. Maybe she wouldn't find work in Greece in her profession as an engineer in. Alone, in the train compartment, she could let her mind wander. Until then, all her thoughts were revolving around the family and leaving them behind. Now she could think about herself and about her future.

If she couldn't find a job what was going to happen to her and her family? She knew from all her reading and the history and economics classes she had taken, that Greece was not an industrial country. The thought suddenly came upon her. Her stomach churned as if she was about to jump headfirst into a bottomless pit. It was the second time she'd had this uneasy feeling in her stomach.

The first time she'd had butterflies in her stomach, was when her colleague, Babiciuc, from her office in Bucharest, announced that he and his wife were going to leave Romania to emigrate to Canada. It had been six months ago, in January, when her colleague finally obtained legal papers to leave.

At that time she knew nothing of the decision she would make six months later, that she too would leave Romania for good. Her colleague was leaving with his wife, and they had relatives waiting for them.

When Silver departed, she left by herself with no definite plans. She took her mother's word that once she arrived in Greece and joined their relatives everything would be fine. She only had to wait until all the family arrived in Greece, and they would live happily ever after.

The train arrived in Athens around 6:00 a.m.. It was still dark. The train station seemed huge and full of people, even at that early hour. From the open window, Silver looked down at the platform. She recognized Marula and waved.

Marula hadn't changed. Silver had met her several years ago when Marula had come to visit them in Bucharest. She was chubby, with beautiful curly blond hair and a wide smile. Her husband stood next to her. He was tall, slim, and handsome, with dark skin and hair. He had a mustache.

Chapter 5

Marula

"Marula! Hi, I'm over here." Silver called in her broken English, waiving halfway out of the train's window. Silver's English was very bad. She knew that, but it was the only language with which she could communicate with her cousin, as she spoke no Greek. Silver had taken one year of English at the University in Bucharest during the evenings, the year before she left Rumania. She only knew enough to get by.

"Silver, finally you got here. We've been waiting for an hour, at least. This is my husband, Iani."

"I have a lot of luggage here, with me. I'll need some help to haul it all out."

"We're both coming up to help you." Marula and her husband climbed the steep stairs and into her compartment.

"Let me look at you," Marula said. "Your hair is very fashionable, you know." Marula said in equally broken English.

"So is yours. You always had the most beautiful hair, and you look unchanged." Silver said hugging her.

"How is Aunt Thiana and Mady and Radu?"

"They're all fine and they transmit their best wishes to you and your children and of course Mother is always asking about Taki, her brother. Oh, Mother said to call her the minute I arrived in Athens. I have to find a pay phone and call her immediately."

"We'll call from my house as soon as we get there. I want to talk to Aunt Thiana myself. How was the trip?"

"Long. Too long."

"Here, we'll help you with the luggage. Iani has his car parked outside the train station."

The three of them hauled her luggage outside the compartment and down the steps of the train to their car, a small beat-up orange Citroen parked outside the station.

Exhausted, Silver could not wait to finally sleep in a bed. It was still dark. Sleepy, Silver glanced at the view as they drove away from the crowded train station. She noticed the large paved boulevards, the white monumental and ornate buildings in the center of Athens. As they approached Marula's neighborhood the cobblestone streets became narrower and steeper. Clusters of three and four story buildings crowded both sides of the streets.

They arrived at Marula's apartment, in an older four- floor building located not far from the center of Athens.

Marula lived in a three-bedroom apartment with her husband and her two small children.

They offered Silver the spare bedroom, which doubled as the family room, because the family's only TV set was there.

"Iani is leaving now to go to work. He's working in a factory that manufactures "mayos", bathing suits. He's a salesman over there. He makes good money."

"What about you? You used to work."

"Yea, I used to work in an office. I type quite fast. But now, since I had my first child, Vanghelitza, I stay home and take care of the children." They were having a cup of coffee in the small kitchen. They called Silver's mother, and talked with everybody in turn.

"And where are the children? I want to see them."

"They're still asleep. It's too early to wake them up. You'll see them later. Now, you better go to bed yourself. You look exhausted."

That night, at about eleven o'clock when she woke up, Silver opened all her luggage and showed Marula the things she brought with her. The clothes and jewelry, all her personal treasures, the perfume bottles and the little Chinese figurines.

"Here, choose whatever you like from my treasures. Choose one of the Chinese jade figurines. And also a fine handkerchief." Silver said to Marula as a sign of goodwill.

"I also brought some china with me. Mother said that I could sell it here, in order to support myself for a while until I'll find a job."

"We need to talk about that. Of course, first you need to work on your papers here. You must get the "right to work" form from the Police. Then, of course is the language."

"I don't know any Greek. I might understand something but I cannot speak it. I can't write or read. There is a different alphabet than the Latin alphabet I'm used to."

"Well, you'll have to start English classes in September, when I come back from vacation. In August we all go to the mountain village, to Avdela, for the summer. Nuly and my husband Iani don't go. They have jobs here in Athens.

"I suppose, I'll stay here?" It was a tentative question. She did not hear Marula extending the invitation for her to go to Avdela.

"You have to work on your papers here, to report to the Police. You'll stay with Null, downstairs."

"That'll be good." I have to straighten out my situation here first, that's right."

"Back to the English classes, Null took them few years back and he said they were very good. If you know English you don't need to know Greek. You'll find some work. And then when you become a rich engineer here in Athens you'll have to remember me, the poor relative. Tomorrow morning we'll go to visit my mother's downstairs."

Plans were made for her. Silver felt as if she was not in control of her life any longer. Somebody else made decisions for her. She was depending on somebody else. For food and sleep and all her needs. That was a different feeling altogether. She was living with her family back home in Romania, but she always made her own decisions. She did not feel she depended on anybody. She had had her own money since she was eighteen years old, a student. She earned a merit scholarship based on her good grades. And after she graduated she had her salary. She was independent. Now, all of sudden she became dependent on somebody else for all her basic needs. Food and sleep. She did not like it.

On the last trip to Greece, her mother had deposited some money in the bank for Silver to have when she arrived. Not much, Silver knew, but enough to give her a start.

Silver had a key to the deposit box where her funds were, at the bank of Piraeus. Her mother's younger brother, Vangheli also had a key.

*   *   *

Downstairs in the same apartment building Marula's parents and her brother Null lived in a two-bedroom apartment in the basement. Silver could converse in Armina or Vlaha with Marula's parents, Taki, her uncle, and Vanghelitza, his wife. They were both from Avdela, the village her mother was from, and they spoke Armina or Vlaha or Macedonian. Silver had learned the language from her grandmother, Maia.

Marula had the better living arrangements; her apartment was on the second floor of the building. There was a back stairway interconnecting the two apartments and Marula was in her mother's kitchen quite often. She was able to leave the children with her.

Then Marula was free to go shopping, have her hair done, meet with friends, or go to the open market.

When the time came for her husband to come home from work, she would cook and have lunch with him. Marula had met her husband in high school and married him immediately after both of them had graduated. They went to England for a year where they learned the English language. That had been the fashion for young people at that time. Silver soon discovered that Marula's and her husband's English was very poor.

Chapter 6

Nulli

It was the first of July when Silver arrived in Greece, and by the middle of that month, her cousin Marula and Marula's children and parents were leaving for Avdela to spend the summer there. They owned a summerhouse in the mountain village where Marula's father and Silver's mother had been born.

The weather in Athens was extremely hot during the summer. Only the men who were working remained in Athens; the wives, children and the older people spent the summer in the villages and islands where they originally came from. Athens became tourist's territory for the summer.

Silver stayed in Athens with her cousin Null. Because Marula had gone, Silver moved downstairs to her uncle and aunt's apartment. The downstairs apartment was in the basement of the building and had three rooms along a hallway with one bathroom and a kitchen. Silver chose the best room, the room her uncle and aunt lived in. Null slept in the kitchen, on the couch. As Vangheli, her mother's younger brother explained it to her, the understanding was that she would cook and clean house and do laundry for Null while his mother was on vacation.

At first, Silver had mixed feelings about being left behind in Athens with Null. She would have liked to go and visit Avdela. She had heard so much about the village and its people from her mother over the years. She was also unhappy about moving downstairs to what she thought to be less comfortable arrangements, as her aunt had only a cold shower instead of the full bath that Marula had upstairs. But soon she realized that she enjoyed being in charge and making her own decisions, at least on how she spent her time, since she was alone for most of the day. For now all her questions and fears about her future and about her situation in Athens, about her family, took a distant second place in her mind as she enjoyed the present situation. She was content with her role as a housekeeper, or to be more precise, as the lady of the house. In a way, she took a vacation from her habitual worries. She'd always had to think about her family first, to study hard to make good grades, to work hard, to prove herself at the office. Back in Romania, the housekeeping was not her job. Although she and Mady had done the housecleaning on weekends, her main jobs had been her studies and her engineering job. She was a woman working a man's job, in a man's world and had to prove herself. The lady of the house, back home, was of course her mother.

Null had a day job at the flower factory and his own business selling telephones in the evenings. He'd finished college and had a degree in business administration. Handsome, he had dark skin, black hair and eyes, and regular features. He always dressed in sexy, expensive clothes. She noticed as, after all, she was doing his laundry.

Null left in the mornings around 8:30 a.m. and came back around 4:00p.m. for dinner. He freshened up, changed his clothes, and left for his evening business. From there, usually he went with his friends and his current girlfriend somewhere to have fun. He returned home late, the earliest being 11:00 p.m.

Vangheli told Silver that Vanghlitza, Nuly's mother, left her with his son to take care of him. Vangheli told her she was expected to buy food and cook for Null using her own money. Silver never questioned the arrangement. Null never asked about it, or offered any money. He came at 4:00 p.m. and expected his meal to be on the table, and as a matter of routine complained that Silver's cooking didn't match his mother's.

Silver was expected to have clean and ironed shirts and underwear always ready. He never asked Silver if she had the money to buy food or detergent or necessities for the house. That's how his mother raised him, and that was what he expected.

Silver took the task of housekeeping seriously. She really enjoyed it. She started with thoroughly cleaning the house. She polished the white marble fools in the hallway. She figured out that the Clorox bleach did a great job whitening the marble floors. She polished the wood floors in her room and she scrubbed the bathroom. Since she was left alone all day long in the house, she felt like it was hers. She took pride in keeping it sparking clean. It was the first time in her life being on her own. She was the lady of the house. It was just make believe, Silver knew, because her uncle Tacky and her aunt Vanghelitza would be back from Avdela by mid- August and would claim their home once again.

Silver discovered the neighborhood "furnos"- the places next door where they baked bread daily. She learned to prepare the food and arrange it in a tray in the mornings and go to the furnos and leave it there to cook slowly in the big oven, along with trays left from other homes in the neighborhood.

When she came back from her daily visit to her uncle Vangheli's pastry shop in Omonia, she went first to pick up the tray with the cooked meal, a loaf of fresh bread warm from the oven, and a bottle of fresh milk for the next day's breakfast.

On Saturdays, the farmers from around Athens would come to each neighborhood and open the fresh product market called "laiki" from early in the morning to about 11:00 a.m. When the farmers left, they left behind the produce they did not sell during the morning. That was for the poor and homeless who cleaned up the tables. Silver went to the laiki every Saturday morning and picked up fresh eggs and salad, vegetables, and oranges and lemons.

She discovered the neighborhood supermarket, a small shop full every imaginable product, from canned foods to detergents and necessities, fresh ham and pastrami and cheeses to dried bread, fresh butter and honey. She also discovered the pastry shop on Odos Panipestimiu where they baked fresco pasties each day, the Greek baklava and sarailie, cattaiff and fresh zureck.

It all seemed so easy, so natural, as if she lived all her life there. As if she had walked on those narrow steep streets all her life, as if she had shopped in those shops all her life. She knew enough Greek to ask for what she needed. She learned the neighborhood streets by simply walking and finding where they led to, every day expending her trips. Strangely it all seemed and felt so familiar to her, even more so than Bucharest, the city she had lived in all her life. There was tranquility to the city and her present life style that Silver could appreciate and enjoy. The tranquility before the storm breaks.

She borrowed the necessary money from her uncle Vangheli with the understanding that as soon as she found a job she would repay him. After all, she had the money her mother had put in the bank the year before as collateral.

Chapter 7

Licavitos

In the morning, after Null left for his job, Silver prepared herself a light breakfast, cleaned the house, and started fixing the food for the dinner. She had bought a fresh cut chicken the day before at the butcher. She had kept it in the refrigerator over night, dressed it, arranged it on a big tray and added small creamer potatoes and whole tomatoes and cut green bell peppers and whole onions in the tray. She poured olive oil on top of the chicken, added black pepper and salt, and covered the tray, ready to take it with her to the furnos on her way to visit her uncle.

Her uncle, Vangheli, had a pastry shop called "Kazino" located on Odos Konstantinou, just off Platia Omonia. On her way back from Vangheli she would stop at the furnos to pick up the tray with the food cooked to perfection. The furnos man did not charge anything for the baking.

Silver set the dinner table around 4:00 p.m. and waited for Null to arrive home. They ate together.

They spoke little during dinner, since their English was so poor.

That evening, after Null had finished his dinner, he asked, "Would you like to go out this evening?" Dark and handsome, he was approximately Silver's age. She knew that if he had not been her first cousin, she would probably have fallen for him.

Silver could not believe her ears. She'd hoped, but thought he'd never ask. Every evening as he dressed up and left, Silver had felt left behind like Cinderella, she thought, laughing at herself. "Yes, sure I would like to go out. I'd like to visit and see as much of Athens as I can."

"I'm going out with friends tonight and maybe you can join us."

"I'd like that. What time are you leaving?"

"I'm going to go to my other business now, and I'll come back by 8:30 p.m. to pick you up. Be sure you're ready."

"I will be!"

Silver cleaned up the table, washed the dishes and started to search through her suitcases. She decided on a fashionable pale yellow blouse and skirt and beige high-heeled sandals. She took a shower, applied her makeup, and dressed for the evening.

At 8:30 Null showed up and took her in his open Jeep. They drove on the narrow streets up a great hill that Null explained was the Licavitos, in the middle of Athens. Paved roads led all the way to the top of the Licavitos and at to two restaurants at different levels, as well as an open amphitheater. People were going to Licavitos by foot and by car. It was a popular tourist attraction.

They stopped at a restaurant. There they met Vangheli, Nuly's friend, and a girl named Kulla. Vangheli was dark, tall, and slender. Vangheli and Kulla were both teachers. Null started to talk to his friend in Greek, leaving Silver and Kulla out of the conversation. Silver liked Kulla right away. She was a young girl, rather small, a little chubby, with beautiful black eyes and shining black hair. She suspected Kulla secretly liked her cousin Null, even though she was engaged to someone else.

Kulla took an interest in Silver and asked her a lot of questions about Romania and her family and the life there. It was a pleasant evening. The air was warm and she could feel the cool breeze from the sea. From the top of the hill, all of Athens could be seen. The spectacle of lights was breathtaking.

When they were ready to leave Kulla said, "Why not ask my brother, George, to take Silver around to show her Athens. I am sure she would enjoy it."

"Are you sure this is a good idea?" Null asked, "I don't want to impose on George!"

"No, it will be fine. I'm sure George will enjoy it too. Just for pareia, camaraderie, Kulla added in an undertone. The two girls exchanged kisses and they all left.

Chapter 8

The "Agapa"

The next morning, while cleaning up the house, Silver heard the telephone ringing. Usually the telephone didn't start ringing until Nuly got home in the afternoon.

"Could I speak with Silver?"

"This is Silver." she said with surprise. Who would call her?

"I'm George, Kulla's brother." George's English was fluent.

"Kulla said you might call."

"I got some tickets tonight to a concert at the Parthenon, would you like to go?"

"Yes! Is it in the open? Where is the Parthenon?" Silver asked quickly, as her excitement mounted. She'd have to know how to dress.

"The Parthenon is an open amphitheater where the ancient Greeks used to have their plays. It is located near the Acropolis. You'll be able to see it! I'll come and pick you up by 7:30 p.m. Is this O.K.?"

"I'll be ready!"

Silver was anxious to meet him, and to go see Athens, the Parthenon, and the people and the way they lived. She wanted to make friends and of course she hoped to find love. She thought George was the same age as Nuly and herself, in his late twenties.

She decided not to cook or go to the furnos that morning. Instead she dressed up and walked to Platia Panipestimiu, a few blocks down from where her relatives lived on Panipestimiu Street.

She brought an already cooked chicken from the rotisseries, which lined the Platia, where the plump chickens slowly browned while rotating on a stick above an open fire and everything was displayed in the windows. There was no time to cook, or visit with her uncle for that matter.

When Nuly came home she told him about George calling and inviting her out. He did not comment except to say that he had plans for himself.

"Is George trustworthy?" Silver asked.

"He's a true gentleman, you have nothing to worry about. He has an important job."

Once Nuly left for the afternoon and probably the evening too, Silver hurried and cleaned up the table, washed the dishes, and put the remaining roasted chicken in the refrigerator. Perhaps it would be enough for tomorrow's dinner too.

She went in her room and pulled the suitcase from beneath her bed. She was pondering if she should wear the long voile pink dress she made just before she left Romania. It was dressy. On a sheath of pink satin there were superimposed layers of pink voile at different lengths. The dress was too pretentious for outdoors, even a concert, she decided.

Maybe she should wear her folk dress. It was floor length, but it was a simple gown of white sheer cotton, with red embroidery at the bosom and hem. It was sleeveless with an embroidered girdle.

Silver decided on the folk dress.

She took a shower and dressed carefully for the evening. She decided on the lavender eyeshadow. Surveying herself in the full-length mirror, she decided she looked her best. The gown showed off her slim figure.

She was so anxious. Ready for an adventure. Ready to meet a new person, ready to see exciting, new places that she had only read and fantasized about. Ready to live her life that had been held for so long on a tight leash. She had been confined by the family tradition and beliefs, by the austere regime, by the continuous study and work, by her duties or whatever she perceived to be her duties towards her family and herself.

Silver answered George's knock. Her heart raced foolishly, for no apparent reason. George was a handsome young man with electric blue eyes framed by red wavy hair and beard. He looked like Neptune, the Zeus of the Sea, tall and slender with straight Grecian nose and fine features.

Silver shook her surprise and welcomed George inside. He gazed at Silver with deep, intense eyes. A light shone deep inside his eyes, as if he recognized her from time spent together in a past life.

They stayed in the hallway, for a long moment staring without saying a word. Silver's breath caught in her chest. Finally, she broke the silence.

"Am I dressed appropriately for the occasion?"

"Definitely. By the way, we're going to an outside festival agapa instead of the concert I promised you. The concert lasts too long, and I have to work tomorrow."

They left and Silver closed the door carefully behind them. George had a black car, Silver could not recognize the make. It looked used and had a sunroof, which was open. They went to the agapa and there they met some friends of George's.

George started to talk to her in rapid English, "Are you visiting Greece and your cousins here in Athens?"

"Yes." Silver answered.

"How long are you going to stay? Do you work back in Romania?"

"I don't know yet. It depends. Yes, I work back in Romania. I am an engineer. What about you?"

"I work for a company here in Athens. I am a supervisor. Not fun. A lot of responsibility. While everybody leaves at 5:00 p.m., I have to stick around and check that everything is O.K. before I leave."

"Did you study here in Greece?"

"Yes. I finished my bachelor degree in business administration and then I went to the United States for my master's. How do you like Athens so far?"

"I've not had a good chance to see much of anything yet."

"We will fix that. Do you like the beaches?"

"Yes, a lot. We have the Black Sea, back in Romania, and we used to go there every summer for vacation."

"We will go to the beaches."

Finally, they arrived. It was a place outside of the city, decorated like a wine festival. There were rustic wooden tables and benches arranged, where food and wine were served. People danced in circles holding hands. George and Silver joined them. Silver stepped all over herself trying to keep up with the intricate steps of the Greek dances.

Later they left, and George bought her home. It was around 11:00 p.m. In the car, George stretched out his hand and clasped Silver's in his. They remained quiet, both engrossed in their own thoughts.

As they drove through Athens that evening, Silver gazed through the window. She felt that the ancient city pulsed alive, like a giant creature. People walked on the streets, crowded the restaurants, occupied all the outside tables on the sidewalks.

Silver thought that the very air in Athens was an aphrodisiac. Athens was the city of lovers.

*   *   *

The house was in complete darkness. Nuly was not home yet, and she slipped into her bedroom and closed the door. She could dream about the night and analyze how she felt about George. She could relive the magic moments again, at her leisure. They were captured in her heart. She really liked George. No, not really. More than that. She knew she could fall in love with him. It was something strange about her. Once she glanced at a man, she knew right away if she could love him or not. Just like that. She knew. Just by looking into his eyes. What the man thought, if he was interested in her or not, if other men fell for her and she didn't care about them, that was all together another story.

George and she had not spoken to each other a lot, or revealed much about each other. She did not know even the simplest fact about George, whether or not he had a girlfriend. But she knew she liked him. The possibility for her to fall in love with him was there.

Not that she fell in love easily. Not at all. Au contraire. There were very few men she set her sights on. Very few she felt she could love. But all that she decided from the very beginning of a relationship. Very foolish indeed. Her feelings and emotions ran deep as a deep lake with a smooth surface. No one would have guessed just by looking at her meek appearance and proper behavior what a volcano of emotions she held inside. Her pride ran even deeper.

Chapter 9

Odos Ermou

The next morning George called again, "This is George, how are you?"

"I'm fine! Thank you for taking me to the agapa last night. I had a good time."

"That's good. Would you like to go to the beach on Saturday? I'm working only half a day Saturdays and after work I can pick you up at the house."

"I would love that!" "I'll come by at noon."

He called. That was a good sign. Maybe he liked her as much as she liked him. Silver's heart sang with joy and she started dreaming with her eyes open. She'd have to think what to wear to the beach.

Silver hadn't packed a bathing suit when she left Romania. That had been the farthest thought from her mind.

That morning, when she went to visit with her uncle Vangheli, she asked him to lend her additional money to buy a bathing suit and asked where to buy one. Vangheli laughed. The Greek beaches were open year around and were the main attraction for tourists as well as the locals. Everybody owned several bathing suits. Greece was famous for their manufacture. Whole stores were dedicated to bathing suits in Athens.

Silver and Uncle Vangheli kept close tabs on the money Silver borrowed. Not that she thought for a moment she would have to use the money that her mother had deposited in the bank for her. She expected to resolve her situation with the papers soon and be able to find a job in Athens as an engineer. She was on a tourist visa with the clear intention to apply for political asylum in Greece as soon as Marula returned from her vacation in Avdela.

She asked her uncle Vangheli, "Will you go with me to 'Thmima Lagapon', since Marula is not here?" It was the central police station in Athens, located just a few blocks away from Vangheli's pastry shop.

Vangheli answered, "I can't close the shop even for an hour. It's simply not done. I'll lose business."

She'd have to wait for Marula since she didn't speak Greek and somebody had to explain what she wanted.

In all fairness, Marula had applied for her tourist visa, not Vangheli.

She took the money Vangheli lent her and went shopping. Vangheli told her to go to Odos Ermou where all the boutiques were. She could not believe the shops' windows and the fashionable clothes displayed in them. Shops lined both sides of Odos Ermou, and just walking down the street and gazing in the windows was enough to make any woman happy. At the end of Odos Ermou was the Monastirachi, the open market for the tourists, where one could buy everything and anything from expensive jewelry to sackcloth and artisans' work.

Also at the end of Odos Ermou was a small, ancient church. The threshold was beneath the street level. Silver had been baptized as a Christian Orthodox as an infant. The Russians, Eastern Europeans, the Greeks, were all Christian Orthodox. The religious customs that Silver had been exposed to back in Romania were basically the same as in Greece. Even though the Communist regime stifled the religion, teaching atheism in schools, people kept the traditions and religious customs, hidden within families, transmitted from parents to children. The faith was strong and religious holidays were observed strictly despite restrictions. It was their inheritance, more so than the land.

Silver went inside the little church. It was dark and cool. Icons framed in massive gold and silver, gloriously hand engraved, adorned the walls. The old woman sitting at the entrance cleaned the trays for the candles. No one was in the church at that time of the morning. Silver knelt in front of the Virgin Mary's icon praying to find her true love, her soul mate. If God willed maybe George would be that person.

After she attended to the matters of the heart, the most important thing, she went into a shop of Odos Ermou and bought a little blue bikini bathing suit with two strings of beads keeping the bottom of it tight together. She liked it. There, she thought, she had the ammunition to conquer George.

Chapter 10

The Beaches

On Saturday, at noon as promised, George showed up at the door. He looked tired and hot. He wore his light gray business suit, but had his blue striped tie loosened.

"It's a nightmare out there in the traffic. Everybody leaves their offices at the same time and tries to get out of Athens to cool off, as soon as possible. One could boil in Athens during summer."

"It's pretty hot."

"I'll stop briefly by my house, which is on the way to the Tallassa-sea, if you don't mind. I need to change my clothes. I came here directly from the office."

"That's perfectly all right with me." Silver answered. They drove in the direction of the sea on the main road leading outside Athens, toward the beaches-"Leouforou Vasilis". It was a wide highway. Cars were jammed one in front of the other and next to each other in all four lanes.

Silver settled back in her seat next to George. George left the car's sunroof open. The breeze blew through it, cooling her heated face.

"You know, I really came here to stay. I mean, I'm going to ask for political asylum," Silver said tentatively.

"Oh. That's a good idea. I know of some people from Romania who came and worked here for a while. They were very poor." George answered. He didn't seem surprised.

"One can't own anything in communist Romania, except the house one lives in. The government controls everything," Silver said. "I have an understanding with my family that after I establish myself, I'll bring them over."

There, she'd spilled the beans. She told him what was in the front of her mind. She needed to talk to somebody about her situation. Marula was on vacation, Vangheli did not offer any help. Nuly was simply too absorbed in his own problems, with his job and his girlfriends, that he really did not ask about her problems let alone discuss them. Yet time was passing and her tourist visa would soon expire.

"My tourist visa is about to expire and I must go to the police station and ask for political asylum. I don't quite know what to expect." Silver continued.

She wanted to get everything out in the open and maybe ease some of her worries. "I asked my uncle, Vangheli, to go with me to the police station, but he refused. I must wait for Marula to come back from vacation. I don't speak Greek."

"I'll come with you." George offered.

Silver turned the thought over in her head. This was a serious matter for her and her family. Her entire future depended on it. She couldn't take chances. She had better wait for Marula. "Thank you for your offer, but don't you have to work Monday?"

"I can take two hours off to go with you."

"That's really nice, but I think I better wait for Marula. This is an important matter and she applied for my visa here. She brought me here. She's talked this over with my mother before hand."

"Whatever you think will work best for you."

Did she imagine it, or was George's voice just a degree colder?

They stopped at the tollgate. There were small booths installed on each lane of traffic. Inside the booth was an attendant, and when a car stopped, he extended a long wooden spoon out to collect the money. Silver thought that was interesting.

She wore her new bathing suit beneath her red tank top and flowery skirt. If the beaches in Athens were like the beaches in Romania at the Black Sea, there would be no place to change clothes.

They stopped briefly at George's house. Silver waited in the car, and then they left for the beaches. They stopped at the first one of the string of beach sites along the coast of the Mediterranean Sea. The place's name was "Vula."

It was a well-organized beach with a gated entrance. The cost of one ticket was not much, forty lepta, but probably enough to pay for the up-keep of the beach. The white sand was clean, freshly combed. There were chaise lounges on the beaches, showers and cabins to change clothes. Very civilized. There were also few restaurants- grills with light tables and chairs.

Silver changed clothes in the cabin, and met George on the beach. He talked with friends, young girls and men, in a big circle.

George introduced her to his friends "This is Silver. She is from Romania. She is visiting her cousins."

They all went to eat a light lunch at the restaurant of hamburgers and French fries drenched in ketchup, and drank cold beer. They were seated around the outside bar on high stools. Later, they stretched out on the chaise lounges on the beach. Silver occupied the chair next to George's.

The girls talked in Greek. Silver could hear them. Everybody assumed she didn't understand what were saying.

She was at that first stage of learning a language when one can understand what was spoken but could not quite speaks it. Years of listening to her mother and her grandmother speak Greek had gotten Silver to that point. Now in Athens, going to the shops and buying groceries she had to ask for whatever she needed using the few words she knew.

"She is pendaomorfa." one girl said, pointing to Silver. Silver knew that "pendaormofa" meant five times more beautiful.

"Yes." replied the other girl, staring with envy at Silvers' slender, athletic body displayed in her tiny bathing suit.

George overheard the remark, because he immediately placed a possessive hand over her shoulders. They went into the water, and Silver found out George was an accomplished swimmer. Silver had taught herself to swim and was certainly no expert. But she followed George out into the deep water.

As the sun slowly descended into the water, the sea itself calmed as well. There were no more waves. They could swim and play, easily splashing water into each other's face. Later they stretched out on the lounges, Silver and George, holding hands and watching the red sun falling into the sea.

How peaceful. As if it was the beginning and the end of the world. Everything and everybody around them disappeared and the two of them were left alone on the surface of the earth. The two of them, the sea, and the sun falling into the immensity of the sea, red as blood.

Chapter 11

George

Silver was quite pleased with her new hairdo. Before she had left Romania she had gone to the most expensive hair salon in Bucharest at the hotel Athenee Palace, a place exclusively for tourists, and had her hair cut short. Her hair was like a halo around her face, accentuating her delicate features. The shorter hair accentuated her hazel eyes and sensitive mouth.

Silver dressed for the occasion. George had invited her to go sailing. She'd never sailed before. She wore her bathing suit with a red halter-top and a flowery skirt over it and sandals on her feet.

Around noon George picked her up. George drove toward the sea. She recognized the route and the residential area near the sea, with beautiful two-story houses.

George stopped in front of a sturdy house surrounded by balconies. George spoke in rapid, flawless English that Silver could understand pretty well. Silver learned from Nuly that George held an important position in the company he worked for. George told her that he needed to hook the boat to his car and she'd have to wait awhile.

"Come on inside." He opened the heavy, ornate front door of the house.

Silver followed him up the marble staircase, all the while wondering about the beautiful, rich house he lived in. They entered a dimly lit hallway that opened into the living room. On the far side was the dining room where the family was eating lunch. George invited Silver to wait in the living room on a sofa. Silver sat down and gazed around in awe. The setting was opulent. Over the fireplace hung a great mirror. Soft rich rugs of burgundy adorned the polished wood floors. The clattering of glasses and silverware came from the dining room. She waited patiently for George. Silver could hear him talking to his parents.

George's mother came into the living room to greet Silver. She was a short, heavy woman with bad teeth and thick glasses. She inspected Silver with a critical eye making Silver feel like an insect pinned on cardboard and examined under a magnifying glass. She wondered if her attire was appropriate. Maybe her halter exposed too much skin. Maybe George's mother thought Silver's clothing was indecent. How did such a beautiful man like George come forth from such an ugly woman?

George's mother didn't address her directly. Probably she thought Silver didn't understand Greek. She spoke to her son as if Silver was a lifeless object. "Do not bring this one in the house every day as if you are going to take her for your bride."

Silver couldn't believe her ears. Her heart sank. Never in her life had she been exposed to or treated with such rudeness. She was speechless and decided to say nothing as if she couldn't understand them.

George stood, next to his mother, and stared at Silver as if pondering her. He said nothing in response to his mother's rude remark.

Silver hoped she hadn't blushed or let her hurt show in any way. She figured out a long time ago that her pride did not allow her to show how deep her feelings were wounded. All her hopes for a romance with George were killed right there by George's mother's words. She understood that these people were not treating her as an equal. She was a foreign object of amusement. Back in Romania where she lived with her family, where she grew up and went to school, where she had friends who knew her, or at the office where she worked as an engineer, nobody, but nobody, would dare treat her like that. It was a total shock for her that people would look at her like a fallen woman. As if she was someone looking for a good catch, for the money or the situation that a guy had in order to get married and be taken care of. As if that was anything like her. If only these people knew her. How could George stay there looking like this as if appraising her, and through his silence in a way agreeing with his mother? What a shame. She hoped for love. The true love one hopes to find once in a lifetime. She hoped for a soul mate, a man of equal intelligence and education, of equal sensitivity. To be treated as such was beyond her imagination.

Chapter 12

George

Finally George's father entered the living room. He was a tall handsome man, and Silver understood where George's good looks came from.

With his hand held out, George's father came forward and greeted Silver in his broken English. He looked worldly and like a true gentleman. "Where are you, pedia, heading out to?" George's father asked in a soft tone.

"We were planning to go to the beach and take the boat with us. Silver has never gone sailing. I think she'll enjoy the experience," George said.

"Why don't you go by your cousins' house on you way to the beach? I think they wanted to go with you sailing today." George's father said.

"That's a good idea. Maybe Aunt Maria would like to go with us too." George said. "Too bad Kulla is not home today. It would have been nice for her to go with us, since Silver already knows her."

On the way to George's cousins' house Silver sat in the car next to George, upright, with her lips tight and her arms crossed across her breasts. She could not look at George nor speak with him. She was so hurt.

George, on the other hand, had no idea there was anything wrong. He talked rapidly in English, not even expecting an answer from her.

They stopped to pick up George's cousins and his aunt while Silver waited in the car.

When George's cousins got in, they all chatted in Greek, totally ignoring Silver. Finally they arrived at the beach. Silver has been to the beaches back in Romania at the Black Sea, but nothing had prepared her for the beauty of the Mediterranean Sea. The sky was an intense, clear, shade of blue. No cloud could be seen. She couldn't remember rain in Greece from the moment she arrived. The sea was a shade of aquamarine, reflecting the incredible blue of the sky and showing the clear, white sand of its beaches.

The weather was much warmer than in Romania at the same time of the summer, but on the seashore one could not feel the warm weather. A cool breeze came from the sea. The water was warm and pleasant for swimming.

George's cousins got busy with a game of volleyball, while the aunt settled herself on the beach and prepared the refreshments she had brought with her. It was late in the afternoon, and the beach was almost deserted.

To Silver's amazement, the cousins and George's aunt proved to be pleasant and all made an effort to include her into the games. The aunt offered her sandwiches to eat and lemonade to drink. It was difficult to be upset with somebody who was so nice.

George and Silver went for a cruise with his motor boat, just the two of them. The others politely declined George's offer. George sped the boat over the water's surface. At this time of late afternoon the sea was smooth as oil. No waves. The sun was going down into the sea, and the sky was a beautiful hue of pink. George cut off the engine and left the boat drift. He had driven the boat far out, and the shore could no longer be seen. He held out his hand and clasped Silver's.

By now, Silver thought, he understood that she was upset, but could not figure out why. George hadn't asked Silver what was wrong. Silver was too stubborn and proud to say something. It was her pride and her hurt feelings. The hurt was so deep, so painful that she could not open up and talk about it. Also she felt that hiding her real emotions, the hurt and humiliation she felt was what she had to do in order to preserve her dignity as a human being. Being hurt and humiliated by others might happen without her having any say in the matter. However not showing the same people how deeply they wounded her was a matter of pride to her. She would not give them that satisfaction. She would play it cool.

Silver turned her head slightly toward George, stealing a glance at him. His blue, electric eyes, framed by the red hair and beard, seemed hurt and puzzled. They were lying on the bottom of the boat, with their heads on the boat's bench, each on either side. Silver glanced at their bodies. The purple light of the sunset made them look like highly polished bronze. Silver felt like they were the only two people left on the earth, lying there between the sky and the sea. The silence was absolute, not broken by even the smallest sound. She could not imagine a more romantic setting, yet her heart was heavy as lead in her chest and ached like a raw wound.

Finally, George turned on the boat engine and they returned to the beach.

It was dark outside when they returned home. First, they dropped the cousins at their house and then they went on to George's.

When they arrived, George insisted Silver come upstairs and wait while he unhooked the boat. Silver refused to go into the house. She felt she had been thrown out of there in the morning and she had no intention of being humiliated again.

George went upstairs and talked to someone, apparently his mother and sister, Kulla, because his mother appeared on the balcony facing the street where Silver was waiting in the car. She made an inviting sign toward Silver to come upstairs into the house. Silver wouldn't move. She was too hurt.

Kulla, George's pretty sister came downstairs and went along with them in the car to drive Silver back home. Silver liked Kulla from the first time she had met her. She was talkative and nice. She resembled her mother, but with a difference. The girl was small and dark, rather heavy- set, but her face was smooth, the color of ivory. Her hair thick and shining black, her eyes, dark brown and soft, like the eyes of a deer.

Silver could not possibly be rude to Kulla. They both started chattering in their broken English. George was relieved. Silver could see that.

Chapter 13

George-The Night Alone

They finally arrived at her cousin's house. Silver said her good-byes and thanked both George and Kulla for the nice day she'd had. Quietly she let herself into the dark house. Apparently Nuly was not home yet. It was too early for him. He was probably out with his friends or his girlfriend having a good time.

She undressed in the dark, and slipped into the bed. The entire apartment was located in the basement of the building. From her room Silver could see the street through the high small window next to the ceiling. Actually, she could see only the feet of the people passing on the street. But now it was night, everybody had retired, and the full moon light filtered through the small window and spilled onto Silver's bed. She lay there in her thin nightgown, slowly releasing the events of the day as if in a slow motion movie she was rewinding. Her heart was heavy with emotions. She was alone in a foreign country among people whom she hardly understood, in a different society altogether than the Communist Romania where she had grown up. The Communist Romania had no social classes and was used to a society where women and men were equal, with the same rights and opportunities. She missed her family, her mother especially. Back in Romania life was not easy, certainly, but her parents sheltered her and her siblings from outside hardship. She grew up in a world she invented for herself, in her ivory tower, where everything was good and beautiful. She read too many novels. That was what was wrong with her. Too many love novels, and her expectations for love were unrealistic and unreasonable. Now, bitterly, she thought how fast she has fallen in love with George.

It had happened before, back in Romania, she had loved a young man. A colleague of hers for years, the young man had not returned her love. What was wrong with her? Maybe each time she had fallen in love with her ideal of a man, with her expectations of what she wanted in a man, superimposed on yet another pretty face. That's why she was falling in love so easily. The less she knew about the man up front, the better he matched her ideal. Maybe she put these men on a pedestal to start with and when they proved less than what she expected she was disappointed and took it out on them.

Remembering the day's events, she realized that she was the one who had behaved like a spoiled child. Everybody, except for George's mother, had been very nice to her. George himself was nice and gentlemanly. She knew, she liked him very much and was on the brink of falling in love with him. Why couldn't she play the game like all the girls she knew back in Romania? Why didn't she play the fool and take the mother's abuse with a smile until she reached the goal of getting her man? Why couldn't she compromise like everybody else? Did she think for a moment that George's mother's remark about her was a casual one, a remark with no consequences? No, she was too smart for that. She knew too much about the Greek customs from her own family. She knew exactly the weight of George's mother remark. This girl does not meet our social status. You cannot take her seriously. She's foreign, she's poor, and she has nothing. She's not a match for you.

Silver knew all that from her mother's stories about growing up poor in Greece. She knew that a man of a certain social position in Greece would expect to marry a girl from a well-known family and expect "prika", dowry, from the girl's family. The higher the man's position in society the more "prika" he expected. But who knows. Would she succeed in conquering George? Maybe. Her head ached.

She would be nice to him tomorrow, she promised herself, and fell asleep.

Chapter 14

George-Good bye!

That morning Silver was agitated. She couldn't stay still. Her heart was heavy. She hadn't felt good about the way she had behaved the night before. She couldn't do anything about the way others behaved, but she was sorry she had been rude the night before. If it was in retaliation for George mother's comment, that was beside the point. She should not have behaved like a spoiled child who had not gotten what she wanted.

She was pacing the long hallway in front of the telephone. She decided if George didn't call by 10:00 a.m., she would call him at his office. She needed to talk to him, to explain.

Finally George called, "I'll pick you up around 8:00 p.m. We'll go for a short ride as I have to leave in the morning with the family for a ten-day vacation."

"That's fine." Silver was taken aback. George had not mentioned anything about going on vacation. She'd be left behind in Athens, alone. She felt betrayed, abandoned. That fueled her opinion that he did not really think of her as more than an acquaintance, his friend's cousin. Why had he not mentioned anything about going on vacation the day before? But in all fairness to George, she'd behaved like a spoiled child. She had not talked to him.

Silver could not eat anything at dinner. If Nuly noticed anything amiss he did not mention it.

Silver could not wait for Nuly to leave. She started to dress up and took pains to look her best.

George showed up at the door and they left for a drive. All her carefully made plans to explain her behavior of the night before and even to apologize collapsed, as she felt George to be distant and cold toward her.

Maybe it was all in her head. Maybe it was her imagination that had overtaken her. Maybe George did look at her as merely an acquaintance. Maybe all the romantic stuff was only in her head. Nothing real. How could she apologize? Maybe she had misinterpreted the rude statement that his mother had made and the rationale behind it.

"I have to drive the family to our house in the islands for a vacation. I'll stay only ten days with them and then come back to Athens. I have only ten days vacation from my job. My parents will stay longer, an entire month.

"And who is going to bring them back? Does your father drive?" Silver asked.

"No, father does not drive. I will bring the car back with me. I need to drive to work every day. When they are ready to come back at the end of the month I will go and pick them up. I still have to pack this evening." George said as if in a hurry.

"Is Kulla going too?"

"No. She stays here, with her fiancée. Did she mention to you that she is to be married this autumn?"

"No, she didn't."

They returned to Silver's cousin's home early. In the car, George kissed Silver good bye. "Are you going to find yourself another boyfriend during the ten days I will be away?"

"I don't intend to." Silver responded in an icy voice. Silver felt hurt. Her heart was heavy, aching with a tangle of mixed emotions. She would have liked to scream, to shake George and ask him if anything was real. If he even cared about her. But she couldn't. She'd not utter a word. It was her pride again. Her perception of conventions, of proper behavior. How could he talk to her this way? Who did he think she was? An easy woman? Did she give him grounds to think so with her behavior? What happened to the gentle, nice George she knew?

George parked the car right in front of her cousins' window, on the abrupt slope, in a precarious position. As George moved over to kiss her Silver felt the car moving. He kissed her hard on the mouth. It bruised her lips.

Something was terribly wrong. George's attitude towards her had changed overnight. She did not recognize the brute next to her.

All her resolutions to explain the night before and to apologize slipped away. Silver froze in her seat.

Chapter 15

Home Alone

Silver was left alone in Athens, with Nuly.

Nuly, as far as she could see, was a ladies man. Girls called him at home all hours of the evening. He was an expert at the game of love, Silver decided. At that particular time he had a steady girl-friend, a doctor named Maria.

Silver waited for him to get home. She set the kitchen table for the two of them. She prepared a leafy green salad and kutopoulos, roasted chicken.

When he arrived home Nuly asked Silver "Did my girlfriend Maria call?"

"Yes, she asked for the telephone number where she could reach you."

"Did you gave her the telephone number for my business?"

"No, I didn't know it. I gave her the number here."

"She knew this one. How else would she have called?"

"I suppose you're right." Silver answered.

"What do you expect me to do now? You can't even give the right telephone number." Nuly was upset.

"I said I was sorry. I suppose you can call her and talk to her." Silver said.

"What do you know. I can't call. I would give her the impression that I like her. I can't do that! She should

call me. I have to make her love me. If I call, she will know I love her."

It was pretty obvious to Silver that Nuly did love Maria. Otherwise he wouldn't get so upset. When the other girls called, he seldom asked anything. He did not care. He did care about Maria.

That was something that Silver had to learn about the game of love. It was an art to make the other person love you.

"Why do you prepare so much salad?" he asked.

"I like salad. That's what we use to eat back in Romania. Don't you like it?"

"I like it but not so much. A whole bowl. And the koutopoulos has too much oil! Mother used to make it better." Nuly said, still upset.

"I'm sorry. I suppose that's the best I can cook!"

"I am going to take a week vacation and visit Maria on the islands, where she lives. Would you like to go with me?"

"I have to stay here." Silver said, as much as the idea of travelling and seeing the country appealed to her.

"Why do you have to stay in Athens?" Nuly asked.

"I do not know yet what to do about my papers and my status here. Also George has asked me to wait for him."

"Are you going to stay here alone in Athens just to wait for George?"

"Yes that's what I want to do. What if he comes back from the islands and he can't find me?"

"Look, this is stupid! You don't wait for a guy." Nuly said.

"Besides, I don't want to spend too much money. Who knows what's going to happen to me?" Silver stood her ground.

"You don't have to worry about money. Come with me!"

"No thank you. I'd better stay here! Do not worry about the house. I can take care of it. I'll be fine."

There was something else that had bothered her for a while. She had to speak with Nuly about it before he left.

"There's something I have to tell you."

"What's that?"

"The other night you were out and I was in the kitchen here downstairs. I was preparing something light to eat before bed. Marula's husband Iani came downstairs and asked me if I wanted to go out."

"And what did you say?"

"I refused. I thought it was very inappropriate for him to do so."

"Was he drunk?"

"I don't know. Maybe, now that I think of it."

"And then what happened?"

"He left, and I went to bed."

"That's O.K. I'm glad you told me about it."

"When is Marula coming back? I need to take care of my papers."

"At the end of the month. So you've decided not to come with me after all."

"I think that I'd better stay here."

Silver was torn between her desire to enjoy herself and go on vacation with Nuly as if she had no worries in the world, and her sense of duty and responsibility that would not let her go. She had serious business to attend to here in Athens that would decide her future. She had to wait for Marula to clarify her situation. She also wanted to wait for George, even though Nuly has advised her against it.

Chapter 16

George-The Confrontation

Now that she was all by herself, Silver started to mind her expenses. She was still borrowing money from her uncle Vangheli. Since she had to worry only about herself, she stopped buying roasted chickens and meat. She bought only eggs and salad and potatoes, oranges and lemons, and bread and milk for breakfast. Her money was going fast and she had not resolved anything yet. A whole month had gone by, and she had done nothing more than spending the money that her mother had deposited in the bank. She had not achieved anything. The thought burned in the back of her mind.

After a week, Nuly got back from his vacation. Silver asked him how things had gone with his girlfriend, but he did not give her any details. He clearly resented her for not going with him. Maybe he thought Silver could help his situation.

The ten days that George had said he would be in the islands with his family had passed too, and Silver waited for George's call every day. She had no way of knowing if George was back. She just had to wait for his call.

One morning, he did.

"Remember me? This is George."

"Of course I remember you. How was your vacation? When did you get back? Is your family back too?" Silver was asking too many questions at once. She was so relieved that he had called, that he was back and had not forgotten her.

"Would you like to go out tonight?"

"Yes. Of course. Where? I mean, how should I dress?"

"I don't know. My cousin and I will be there to pick
you up about 7:30 p.m.."

"That's fine with me! I'll be ready."

Silver had a bad feeling about the conversation. George's voice was cold as if he were talking to a stranger. As if he did not know her.

That evening when Nuly got home from his work, Silver told him about the conversation she had with George.

"Did he say he would bring another man with him?" Nuly asked.

"Yes. He said he would bring his cousin along."

"Did he say he would bring another girl too?" Nuly asked.

"No. He didn't mention another girl."

"What time did he say he would pick you up?"

"About 7:30 p.m. Is there anything wrong?" Silver started to feel very uncomfortable.

"You're not going anywhere tonight."

"Why? What is wrong?" Silver asked, alarmed.

"Did you let George know that you like him in any way?"

"I don't know! I suppose so. He kissed me before he left."

"Did you let him?"

"Yes. Why not? I like him. Why play games? Is anything wrong?" The thought flashed through her mind. She knew from her mother and the way she has been brought up that the Greeks, all Christians really, considered a woman's virtue to be her best asset, that a man expected his bride to be a virgin untouched by other men. With the Greeks it was even more so. It was a question of the family's honor. But was kissing in the same category? Should she not have let George kiss her? Was that what Nuly was talking about? Was that the way she was supposed to act? She had been kissed before. She did not think that was a sin, or proved anything wrong about her morals. What were these people thinking? She certainly didn't have a clue.

"I think he's bringing the other man for you to night. He brought himself a girlfriend back from the islands!"

Silver's heart sank. She could not believe anybody capable of such cruelty. Certainly Nuly was mistaken. George had not mentioned any girlfriend. Maybe he just wanted to introduce his cousin to Silver.

Nuly did not let her dress up for the evening and stayed home with her to wait for his friend's arrival. She was wearing her house robe and no makeup.

Finally George and his cousin, a young boy who was home from the army, entered the house. Nuly and Silver greeted them and invited them to the kitchen to visit for a moment.

"Is Eleni with you today?" Nuly asked in a casual tone.

"Yes. She is waiting for us in my car outside." George answered unruffled.

"You'll have to excuse Silver tonight. She doesn't feel well. She'll not be able to go with you tonight." Nuly offered in a calm tone.

"Ooh! We had hoped to have a good time tonight, but if she cannot come we are on our way out. Good bye then!"

The two men left.

After that Nuly left too. Silver was left alone in the dark house. She went back to her room, slowly undressed, and went to bed. Her heart was heavy and she started to cry all by herself in dark. How dreadful. She could not imagine such cruelty. Thank God for Nuly who had stayed with her. Otherwise she would have gone with them without even knowing that George had his new girlfriend waiting for them in the car. She would have had a hard time adjusting to the situation with no prior notice. Who knows, she might even have become sick and embarrassed herself in front of those people, or she might have started to cry. What kind of people were they? Would she be able to survive among them?

Chapter 17

Vangheli

The next morning, Silver went to talk to her uncle Vangheli, at his pastry shop. Vangheli was the younger brother of her mother. He was selling baklavas and sarailis and candies made by the famous factory "Loutraki". He'd been doing this for most of his life. He was making good money. He was even considered rich by Marula's standards. Vangheli was in his late forties, with silver gray hair that he combed neatly over his head, and a little potbelly.

Silver knew that from being in contact with people on a daily basis he was a good judge of character. Now she wanted to talk with him about George and what had happened the day before. She sat down on the little stool next to the refrigerated display window. Vanghleli stood behind it, watching the open front door for potential customers and listening to her story. "You're guilty of a cardinal sin. You scorned the boy's mother. He'll only marry the girl his mother approves of."

Cold fingers tightened around Silver's heart. He was right, of course. It was her pride and stubborn streak. That's what it was.

"But she insulted me to my face." Silver defended herself. "I didn't want to go back into the house she had practically thrown me out of."

"If you were smart you would've played the fool and made as if you didn't understand, and been nice to the boy's mother. Now everything is over. Move forward. Forget him. Find yourself somebody else."

His mater of fact statement felt like a gravestone over Silver's heart. It was all over. Before it even began.

"Marula is returning from her vacation tomorrow. I suppose I'll have to move upstairs again."

"Make sure you behave." Vangheli warned her.

"I have to go to the IPIA. My tourist visa is expiring."

"Marula brought you here, she has to go with you." Vangheli turned to serve a customer.

Silver went back to her cousin's house, packed, and was ready to move upstairs by the next day.

When Marula arrived she seemed more distant and removed from Silver and her problems. Silver pleaded with her to go to IPIA, the central police station, to help her with the paperwork and translation.

A few days later Marula took her two children and went with Silver to IPIA.

There were thousands of people waiting to talk to the clerks, to apply for tourist visas, to validate their passports. The lines were interminable. Marula's children cried and screamed that they wanted to go home with their mother. Silver took a number and waited patiently, pleading with Marula to also have patience, and trying to calm down the children until her turn. In a flashback Silver thought about George's offer to go with her to the police station in the very beginning. The very thought of George made her heart ache. How stupid she had been to refuse him. Maybe their entire relationship could have developed differently if she had trusted him and accepted his offer to help with her problems. Now every-thing was over. He had gotten himself a girlfriend from the islands, his family's home, a girl that his family knew and liked. How stupid she had been to wait for Marula. Marula seemed to have no time for her, and lately it had seemed as if Marula was withdrawing from her. She did not even have the interest to help Silver with her problems. She had her family to think about, her husband and her children.

The policeman, seated behind the counter, listened carefully to Marula's story. He studied Silver's passport and told Silver to come back in two weeks. They would investigate her request for political asylum. Meanwhile she should go to the Romanian Embassy in Athens and extend her visa, as it was about to expire. It would take time for the Greek police to investigate the matter.

By the big crowd waiting at the police station to get their visas extended and by the cold tone of voice of the policeman behind the counter who took her papers, Silver realized that receiving political asylum from the Greek government would be a difficult problem. Mother had assured her that it was as simple as asking for and receiving it.

And she had believed her mother.

Chapter 18

MARULA-The Confrontation

Silver knew something was wrong the moment she opened the door. The house was strangely quiet for that hour in the afternoon. Marula's husband was not home yet. She couldn't hear the children playing. Something was definitely unusual.

Silver had been out in the streets since morning, and had just enough to eat to get by. In the mornings Marula offered breakfast. Silver had breakfast at the kitchen table with Marula and the children. After that, Silver would visit her uncle at the shop or visit Maria, or simply window-shop. Lunch and dinner were up to her entirely. Marula prepared meals for her husband and ate with him when he returned from his job, usually around five.

Neither Silver nor the children were included. Marula had never invited her to lunch or dinner and Silver could not bring her self to look in the refrigerator for food. Marula had never mentioned that it was O.K. for her to do that. She felt like a guest in Marula's home, and more often an unwelcome guest. The children had their meals downstairs with their grandmother, Vanghelitza. Silver knew the rules and usually sneaked into her room and took a nap. Later in the evening Silver would go out again.

Usually she brought a Souvlaki sandwich from the shops lining Platia Omonia. The sandwiches were tasty enough, though rather expensive. Her funds were limited and she had already spent a good portion on buying food for Nuly while his mother and sister were on vacation.

Silver tried to sneak unnoticed into her room. She was hungry and exhausted from spending the day in the streets. She tried not to interfere with Marula's life, or be a burden to her.

Marula was waiting for her in her room. She held the letter Silver had received from her mother in Romania.

"Your mother is a two-timer. A no good woman. I just knew it! Everybody told me not to mess with her!"

"What are you talking about?"

"Your mother. I found the letter your mother sent you."

"How did you find it?"

"It was in the English dictionary you keep on the table."

"Did you search through my things?"

"Not me but my cousin who spent the night in your room. He knows Romanian! I went this morning to have the letter translated, to make sure I understood!"

"Why? What did you understand?"

"That your mother is trying to trick me into keeping you here without sending me what I asked for."

"What did you ask for?"

"I asked your mother to buy me a new white china service and she writes in the letter that she has no intention of doing so."

"Maybe she doesn't have the money to buy what you want right away. Why don't you choose what you like from the things I brought with me? I brought some china."

"I don't like what you brought! I asked specifically for a white fine china set."

"My mother doesn't have the money right now. She will send it to you later."

"No. She is trying to trick me into keeping you here with no money. She wants to destroy me and my husband, the same way she destroyed my father back in 1947. My husband will lose his job because of you, just like my father!"

Marula finally got to the root of the problem. By now both of them were shouting at each other, their arms making wild gestures as they talked. They were facing each other standing next to her bed. Silver noticed Marula's flushed face, her angry eyes. Silver felt perspiration sliding down from her armpits in little rivulets.

"And how did my mother destroy your father?"

"She married a xenos, a foreign man, and because of that my father lost his job as a judge. Do you have any idea how hard it was for my mother to raise my brother and me without my father having a job? Do you know that after the war when my brother and I were babies, she had to soften dried bread in her mouth to feed us so we could survive?"

"And who told you my mother was responsible for your father not keeping his job and supporting his family? Do you think we had an easy life back in Communist Romania? Do you think we had it easy? Didn't your mother work? My mother always worked."

"Do you want my husband to lose his job too, because of you?"

"Marula, you were the one who signed the papers for me to come here. You promised my mother you were going to help me get established here."

"Yes, but now I cannot keep you here any longer. I cannot risk my husband losing his job. This is the last night you can sleep here."

"And what am I supposed to do?"

"I don't know. Go and stay with your uncle Vangheli. He is rich."

"Would you please give my mother's letter back? I keep all my mother's letters." Silver knew her relationship with Marula was over. They might speak, but nothing would ever be the same. She could never forget the words Marula hurled at her about her mother. Never!

Funny, Silver thought later, how the English words had come so easily during the argument with Marula. The same thing had happened for Marula. Until that evening, Silver thought Marula's English was poor, to say the least. During the argument, Marula spoke English with no difficulty. Amazing how the mind works under pressure.

Totally exhausted, Silver retreated to the quietness of her room after Marula left. She was shaking badly. What was going to happen to her? Where would she go? She knew for a fact that she was not going to live with Marula after what had happened that day. How would she survive in a foreign country with no money, no job, and not knowing the language? What if Vangheli would not take her in? Then what? She had to discuss the matter with her mother right away.

Chapter 19

The Telephones

Silver couldn't sleep that night. Things were getting serious. She needed to gather all her wits about her. She had to plan all her moves carefully. She'd call her mother the next morning to discuss the matter with her and see what should be done. For now, she had to gather all her things from Marula and make sure she did not leave anything behind. She might need everything she owned to survive.

There was no doubt in Silver's mind that she had to move out. But where?

Again, in times of need and crisis, her pride came to her rescue. She called it her pride but maybe it was her inner strength. That power, that determination that came from within. In times of crisis, even back home when a member of the family got sick, or when she was facing hard exams in college, or back in 1977 when the big earthquake hit Bucharest, it was like her body gathered all her strength and she became calm and alert. Her mind worked fast, with precision, making the right decisions. She'd survive. She knew it!

The next morning, as soon as the daylight crept through, Silver got up without any noise and dressed up quietly in her room and left the house. She walked to Platia Omonia. There, in the subway station beneath the Platia were the public telephones. She could call her mother directly in Bucharest if she had enough coins.

She had the privacy of talking to her mother without charging the long distance bill to Marula's phone.

"Mother. Hi. It's me. I have problems." Silver shouted from the top of her lungs in the empty subway station.

"Hi. I am glad you called. What happened?" Silver's mother asked. Her voice came through clear and dear to her, as if her mother were sitting next to her.

Silver missed them all so much, tears slid down her cheeks. "Marula threw me out of her house."

"Why, what happened?" Mother sounded upset.

"She found the letter you sent me and decided you are trying to trick her," Silver answered in a muffled voice.

"That can't be it! There has to be more than that. What happened?"

"She told me she's afraid her husband would lose his job because of me living with them."

"Where are you now?"

"I'm in Platia Omonia at the automatic telephones." "Calm down. Go to your uncle Vangheli and tell him

what happened. He'll take you into his house, I'm sure."

"I'll do that. It's too early yet. Vangheli's not at his shop. I'll wait outside until he comes. How's everybody at home?"

"Fine. Don't worry about us. Solve your problem. Stop crying, that won't solve anything. We're all sending our love to you and are behind you one hundred percent. Call me and let me know what you and Vangheli decide."

Silver calmed as if an angel had toughed her very soul. Everything would be fine. Her mother was right; she was not among strangers. She'd probably prefer living with Vangheli's family rather than with Marula's anyway.

She walked down to Vangheli's shop and waited for him to come to his job.

Chapter 20

Vangheli

Vangheli was her mother's younger brother, maybe ten years younger. He lived in Aghia Paraskevi, the new fashionable suburb where rich people were building policatekias- multi-floors buildings. Her uncle owned an entire floor in a new policatekia in Athens. He also owned houses in Dadi, his wife's natal village, and Avdela, Vangheli's family's town.

Silver waited patiently until about 10:00 a.m. when Vangheli arrived.

"What are you doing here this early in the morning?" Vangheli asked while unlocking the front door and pulling up the metallic nets from the windows. He started arranging the big bags with multi-colored candies just outside the open front door, on the sidewalk, so it would tempt the tourists and they would came inside the shop and buy something.

Silver moved past him inside the narrow, dark shop. "Marula doesn't want to keep me any longer at her house," Silver began.

"Oh."

"I talked to mother over the phone this morning and she told me that you would take me in to live with you and your family!" Silver said, getting directly to the heart of the matter.

"That's nonsense." Vangheli said, still with his back to her. "I can't take you into my house. I have young children still in school. I can't jeopardize their future for you." Vangheli said.

"Where am I supposed to live? What am I supposed to do?" Fear overcame Silver.

"I don't know." Vangheli turned around to face her. "You do that which you set out to do when you came here. Did you think you could live with Marula or me forever?"

"I don't know. My mother told me I could stay with you or Marula, otherwise I wouldn't have left Romania." Silver could not recognize her own voice. It was sharp like a razor blade, echoing the chill rising inside her.

"You stayed three months at Marula's. How long did you think you could remain there?"

"I stayed one month and a half downstairs with Nuly and fed him out of my own money. I cleaned the house and washed his clothes."

"And why do you think they let you stay there? Exactly that. To take care of Nuly and the house while Vanghelitza was in vacation."

"But I spent the money that my mother left in the bank for me to feed him. You told me to do that." Silver shouted.

"Otherwise they wouldn't have kept you there so long."

"But what am I suppose to do now? I can't stay with Marula one more night." Silver felt like crying.

"You could go back to Romania, or move into an apartment of your own."

"But I don't have the money to pay for the rent. I don't have a job yet!"

"That's your problem. What you set out to do when you decided to come here, that's what you'll do! I had nothing to do with your visa."

"How can I find an apartment to rent?" Silver's throat tightened; she could hardly speak.

"You go back home to Marula's and don't reproach her for anything. Ask her to help you find a garsoniera, an apartment, in the neighborhood. I have to attend to my business." Vangheli turned to attend to a customer.

Chapter 21

Packing

Silver turned her back on Vangheli and his shop, and walked back to Marula's. It was evident from the discussion she'd had with Vangheli that Marula had talked to him about her. They'd all decided what to tell her.

She was alone. She had no relatives here, only strangers. True, she had known these people only from the letters sent back and forth over the years and the visit Marula made to Romania back several years, and the few visits Vangheli made to Romania. She had believed her mother one hundred percent. Maybe Mother filtered everything, including her relatives, through her love for them and for her homeland. Mother had transmitted down to her, over the years, her own desire to come back and live in Greece. But Silver's experience was totally different. She felt as if shutters were closing down on her heart. Her childhood, or what was left of it, was gone.

Silver opened the front door and let herself into the quiet house. She knew Marula and the children were napping at this time of the afternoon.

She went directly to Marula's living room and took the expensive Chinese vases she'd brought with her from Romania from Marula's China cabinet. She packed all the china she'd brought with her back into their original boxes. She took her hand-embroidered coat, the folk one, from Marula's armoire.

She went to her room and quietly packed all her belongings, closed and locked her suitcases, and put them under her bed. Silver did not want to leave Marula any gifts. She had paid for her stay. Vaguely, she remembered she'd forgotten to eat that day. It did not matter.

Exhausted she went to bed and slept until the next morning. When she woke she offered no explanations to Marula. Quietly and politely she asked Marula to go with her to find a garsoniera to rent in the neighborhood.

Marula did not speak either. If she noticed the absence of Silver's things from their place in her china cabinet, she did not say anything. She fed the children, put them carriage, and they all went to find an apartment for Silver.

Silver decided she could only afford a rent from 4,500 drachmas a month to no more than 5,000 drachmas. There were very few places she could afford to rent and all of them were dark humid little holes in the basements of buildings. Silver could not fathom living in any of them. They were depressing places where the sun did not shine.

Her family's home back in Romania was a small palace, with large airy rooms, high heavily ornate ceilings, and tall sunny windows.

Silver felt she had reached the bottom of the pit. Mother and her family back in Romania could not help her now. She was all alone in a foreign county. Nobody to talk to, nobody to help her, nobody to turn to. As dark and gloomy as her outlook in life was right then, Silver's belief in God never left her. She knew deep inside that if nobody else helped her, God would never forget her in her time of need. God would protect her and bring her unharmed to a safe landing. Deep inside she was convinced of it. She just had to put her life into God's hands and let him direct her to safety.

Chapter 22

The Garsoniera

Finally Silver and Marula and the children came up to a tall sturdy building on the corner, located on the hill at the foot of the road leading to Licavitos. Marula had heard that there was an apartment for rent in that building. The building itself seemed too elegant for an apartment as cheap as Silver was looking for. Groups of buildings close to each other lined both sides of the clean, very steep and narrow street. They were sturdy buildings of up to five floors tall, with thick stone walls and wrought iron balconies with heavy ornate steel and glass doors.

Marula rang the bell of the security system installed by the front door and asked to speak to the landlady.

Somebody upstairs pushed the button of the intercom system and the heavy front door opened. They entered a neat hallway with a pink marble stairway leading upstairs.

An old and distinguished looking woman dressed in black greeted them at the first floor. They entered the garsoniera that was for rent.

Silver could not believe her eyes. The room was big and sunny, with gleaming hard wood floors. A wide French door lead to a little balcony facing the street. The ceilings were high and the room full of sun. Quite elegant.

Next to the main room were a full bathroom and a small kitchen.

Marula asked, "How much is the rent?"

The old lady sat down in a chair, put her cane next to the chair and started to ask Marula about Silver.

"Who is this young lady and what is she doing here in Athens?"

"She's an engineer from Romania and she'll soon find employment here in Athens. She's my cousin and I guarantee that she is a responsible person." Marula told her.

"Of course my daughter Teresa owns the place and she determines the rent, but I think it is 5,000.00 drachmas a month including water and electricity." the old lady responded.

It was a dream come true, Silver thought. It was the answer to her prayers.

The old lady questioned Marula more about Silver's situation. "How long does your cousin intend to stay in Athens? This place is rented by the year, not by the month."

"Silver is hoping to stay in Athens and is working on her papers for political asylum." Marula answered.

The old lady said, "My daughter Teresa is a very good woman. Not because she is my daughter, but because she has helped a lot of people in need. She will help your cousin with her papers. My husband was a general and we have good connections with the police."

Silver could not believe her luck. It was God's hand, she just knew it. As little Greek as she knew, Silver could distinguish the cultured accent of the old lady, her aristocratic features and the quality of her clothes.

Silver remembered what her mother used to say about the Greek language. There was the popular language spoken by the common people, there was the cultured language one learns in school, and there was the theological language spoken and learned by the priests.

"Now if you like the garsoniera and want to rent it, please give me 10,000 drachmas for two months rent so I know you are serious about renting the place."

"I'll bring the money right away, in half an hour." Silver cut in quickly in her poor, broken Greek.

On their way back, Marula commented "Her daughter Teresa owns half of the building including your garsoniera. Her mother owns the rest of the building. I heard Teresa's husband left her for another woman. That's what's happening to those smart, educated women. They cannot keep their husbands."

Was that a jab to her situation as a single career woman? Silver wondered with resentment.

Chapter 23

The Safe Deposit Box

Marula and the children went back to their home, and Silver ran to the bank to pick up her money. The Bank of Piraeus, where her mother had deposited her money the year before, was located in Platia Omonia. It took Silver about twenty minutes of nearly running to reach the bank. In the basement of the bank were the safe deposit boxes. Agitated, she asked the bank's clerk to open the heavy steel door of the safe deposit room. She took out her safe deposit box from its place and walked to one of the small secluded rooms on the side, where she could search in privacy for her treasures. Since her arrival she had also deposited all her jewelry into the safe deposit box.

Silver started counting her money and with utter dismay noticed that a third of it was missing. The money she owed to Vangheli, she thought, feeling as if a sharp knife was cutting through her heart. He had come and taken his money using the second key to the safe deposit box. He hadn't even told her beforehand.

What a horrible thing to do. Especially now, when she was down at the bottom of the pit. Certainly she could not trust anybody. She was raised to respect her elders, and Vangheli was her mother's brother and her uncle. Not any longer, Silver thought. That's why he is rich, she thought bitterly. He seizes every opportunity to make money. He does not give anything to anybody, relatives or strangers. Mother had always talked fondly of him, her little brother. Whenever had he become like that? A shark. What the love of money and material possessions could do to person's character.

Silver took 10,000 drachmas out of the box, wrapped everything carefully back in her handkerchief, and put her safe deposit box back in its place in the steel wall. She left the bank and walked back to the building. She found the old lady and paid her the 10,000 drachmas for the two months rent. She was safe now. She had a place to live. She returned to Platia Omonia to see her uncle Vangheli, this time her steps heavy like lead, her heart even heavier.

"You took the money that I owed you from my safe deposit box." Silver stated. Her voice sounded heavy. She knew her countenance was as dark as her soul.

"That was my money." Vangheli said in a high pitched voice.

"True enough. It was your money. Now we are even. I don't owe you anything more." Never in her life had she thought she'd have the courage to confront anybody, much less her uncle.

"That's true."

"Then please give me my second key to the safe deposit box. You have nothing to do any longer with my money." Silver said. There for the first time in her life, not counting her fight with Marula the other day, she had been firm. She had stood her ground, and spoken clearly about what was on her mind. She had overcome her shyness. She had broken out of the cocoon of politeness and convention, of how others expected her to behave. She finally had shown what was she made of. These people would never intimidate her any longer.

Vangheli took the key out of his pocket and handed it to Silver.

"Make sure you don't tell your mother all this."

"And why not?" Silver turned her back on him and walked away.

She felt as if a chapter of her life was ending. As heavy hearted as she was at that moment, Silver felt the spring of joy entering her soul like a ray of sunshine. She had risen from the ashes and grown wings of her own, like a phoenix.

She went directly to the pay phones in the subway station and called her mother and told her everything. Her mother refused to believe what she said about Marula and Vangheli's behavior towards her. They were her relatives, her blood. It was too hard for her mother to accept reality. Her memories from her childhood, her brothers, her homeland. All was sacred in her soul. Nothing could have gone wrong with them in the time that had passed since she had left Greece.

Chapter 24

Teresa

It was the next morning when Silver finally met Teresa, her land-lady. Silver was in the process of washing the windows, climbing precariously on the only chair in her new apartment.

Marula and her husband had helped carry her luggage over yesterday afternoon. Marula loaned her a twin steel folding bed that had seen better days, a folding table, and a chair. That was all the furniture Silver had in her apartment.

Silver heard a soft knock at the door and answered.

"Please come in. The door is unlocked."

Silver saw a head peeking around the door with dark wavy hair sprinkled with gray, huge dark eyes, and a broad white smile. A woman in her early forties entered the room.

Still standing on the chair, a clump of old newspapers clenched in her hand, Silver said, "Hi, I'm Silver."

"Yasoo." Teresa answered in Greek. "I am the landlady. My mother told me you rented the place yesterday!"

Teresa's language was cultivated. She spoke slowly and pro-nounced the words clearly for Silver's benefit.

"Yes, your mother told me about you yesterday."

"And what exactly did she say?" Teresa asked, sounding amused.

Silver answered, immediately picking up on the friendly tone of voice Teresa was using. "She said you are a very good woman. She said you might help me with my papers and my situation here." Silver used her best Greek/English/Romanian combination.

"That doesn't sound like mother." Teresa smiled. "I see that you've established yourself here. I'll bring you a side table that I have no use for."

"Thank you. I could use more furniture." Silver said.

"Please feel free to come upstairs and visit with me and my daughter Rania anytime. It's just the two of us now. My husband is away in Patra with his job, and mother lives one floor up."

Silver thought she sensed sadness in Teresa's voice when she mentioned her husband. "Thank you so much. I will, as soon as I'm settled." Teresa was a nice, friendly lady. Silver was finally welcomed in Greece and Athens by someone. Silver's disposition had become as sunny as the glowing light entering through the open French doors of the balcony, inundating the entire room.

She needed to buy curtains. She'd go to the Monostirache and find sheer white curtains to hang from the ceiling to the gleaming wood floors. She unpacked her luggage and took out the sheets she had brought with her from Romania and set up the bed. She had to buy a blanket as well. Silver added that to her list.

She unpacked the fine China she'd brought with her and displayed it on the side table Teresa had given her. She should buy flowers. She saw fresh cut flowers at the laiki the other Saturday. They would freshen up the room and nobody would notice the sparse furnishings, Silver thought happily.

Chapter 25

Rania

Silver pondered what to fix for dinner. She could cook French fries or scramble eggs in her small frying pan. She'd bought a small kerosene lamp for her kitchen, a small pan, and an ibric for coffee. The kitchen did not have a stove or a refrigerator. She could not buy anything perishable if she was not going to eat it within the next day. She bought Melba toast she could keep in packages, honey and coffee, potatoes and salads, and fresh eggs. Via the student busses her mother sent her cheese and hard summer salami she could keep in the cupboards of her kitchen.

Once a week on Sundays she was invited to lunch at her uncle Vangheli's, and she took the invitation despite her hurt feelings. She needed the nourishment to be able to survive. She always thought her uncle and his wife Gheorghia invited her to lunch for the benefit of the neighbors, so that they would notice how good they were to their niece.

The day she moved into her garsoniera, Silver promised herself to not spend any more of the money that her mother had deposited in the bank. She needed to find a way of making some money. For now, the Greek police had not given her the legal right to work.

She talked to her mother over the phone and asked her to send her china sets from Romania via the student busses. There was a demand in Greece for good china. She would try to sell it and make at least enough money to pay the rent and eat until she could find employment.

She would ask Vanghelitza, Tachi's wife, who knew a lot of people in the neighborhood, to help her sell her China sets.

She had a two-month period of paid rent and utilities and she intended to use it to gather additional money.

Somebody knocked at the door.

"Come in."

A little girl of maybe twelve years old appeared. She had clear green eyes and a big smile that revealed the gap between her front teeth, and pimples all over her face.

"I'm Rania. Mother wants you to come upstairs for dinner."

"Hi Rania. I'm Silver. Thanks. I was just thinking about what to eat for dinner. Tell your mother I'll be there soon."

Silver searched around for something she could bring with her, as a present to her landlady.

She took a beautiful china bowl she had displayed on the side table, and went upstairs.

Teresa's apartment was located on the third floor of the building. Her mother occupied the fourth floor.

Silver rang the doorbell and entered a beautifully decorated hallway, with black marble floors and French doors opening toward the living room. The sun filtered into the living room through the stained glass of the French doors, giving a friendly yellowish light to the small hallway. It doubled as a library. Books lined the walls, neatly arranged on shelves up to the ceiling. A small desk and a telephone were placed against the front wall, framed by the shelves with books.

"Come in," Silver heard Teresa's voice coming from an adjacent room. "I'm here in the kitchen."

Silver opened the French doors and entered the living- dining room. It was a great room with black marble floors and French doors opening towards a balcony that wrapped around the front of the entire room.

Next to the entrance was the dining room area with a round table and antique chairs. On each side of the French doors leading to the hallway were lamps of antique crystal of different colors. Dark blue and yellow and orange. Above the table hung a huge crystal chandelier made of colored beads of crystal shaped in different forms, matching the lamps. The room was beautiful and tastefully decorated. Toward the far end there was a small sofa, armchairs, and a coffee table.

Silver ventured into the kitchen. She could hear Teresa working, clattering the silverware, and the water running. The kitchen was small, with off-white wood cabinets and a small table and chairs that were off-white etched with green.

"Hi Teresa. I bought you a china bowl from Romania." "Thank you. You shouldn't have."

"It's my pleasure."

"Then thank you." I'm fixing something special for us today. Did you know that I went to Paris to a special school to learn how to cook?"

"That sounds cool."

"Well, I'm cooking fachiets, peas in a special pressure cooking pot. Do you like it?"

"I don't know. I have not had it before."

"Did my mother tell you that I'm a teacher, that I give private lessons to the children?"

"I think she mentioned something like that. What are you teaching?"

"I'm teaching Greek literature and also German." "German?"

"My husband Vasili and I went to Germany to study when we were young."

"What does Vasili do?"

"He's an engineer working for OTE, the telephone company. Now he is in Patra. He was transferred for his work."

"I'm an engineer too." "What kind of an engineer?"

"I'm a civil engineer. As soon as I arrange my situation here and they give me the right to work I'll find a job." Silver announced.

"I can help you with your papers here. I'll introduce you to one of my friends, Mr. Lavranos, who is a lawyer. He works with immigration and has powerful connections in the government."

"That'll be wonderful! I don't speak Greek very well, as you can see, and it is very difficult for me to go to the police station and tell them what I want." Silver had started to speak Greek first with Maria and Pipitza, Maria's sister, whenever she visited with them in their apartment near Marula's building, and learned even more by watching television at their house.

"Don't worry. With me and Rania and Yaya you'll learn Greek in no time."

"I do not have money to pay Mr. Lavranos." Silver added.

"He'll not take your money. He's a very good man and was good friends with my father."

"Fachiets are very good." Silver said, tasting the hot soup.

"Yes they are if one knows how to cook them. It is an art, as I told you."

Chapter 26

❖ ❖ ❖

Maria

Silver rang the doorbell outside Maria's building. It was early in the afternoon around 4:00. Silver knew Maria was awake from her afternoon nap by this hour.

Silver hadn't picked up the custom of afternoon napping. She had never slept in the afternoons back in Romania.

Silver had met Maria a few years ago when she visited them in Romania. Silver's mother was a second cousin of Maria's ex-husband Kotchiu. Maria was now in her late sixties, and was long divorced. However she never ceased loving Kotchiu, even though they could not stay married because of his political convictions. Kotchiu was communist, and involved in the underground organizations. Maria still considered herself married to him and therefore cared about all his relatives, including Silver.

Silver had gone to visit Maria first when Marula left for Avdela with her family, and she had been left alone with Nuly.

Maria's apartment was located one block down from Marula's apartment. From Maria's balcony you could see Marula's street and house.

It was the time for afternoon coffee and cookies, Silver thought. She started to look forward to the little treats she could get at her family and friends' houses.

That in itself was a shame, Silver thought, as it was the love Maria received her with that made her come to visit with the elderly lady.

Maria opened the outside door and Silver climbed the stairs to her apartment. There in the hallway, Maria threw open the door of her apartment. She greeted Silver with open arms. She kissed her and pulled her inside the house. In the living room Maria had small coffee cups on the table, and brought out hot aromatic coffee from the kitchen. She unwrapped fresh coloureds from the boxes her nephews had brought her, to treat Silver. It was so home- like here with Maria, as if she were with her Aunt Maria back in Romania.

The furnishings of the house were old-fashioned, like Maria. There was an old solid oak table in the middle of the room covered with a handmade lace tablecloth, and a sideboard full of family photographs displayed prominently.

Maria was a good-hearted and very religious woman. She and her sister Pipitza and Pipitza's children had embraced Silver as a member of their family and welcomed her every time she stopped to visit.

"I talked to Mimis' mother today." Maria announced very pleased.

"Yes?"

"I told her you need a job. Mimis has an engineering company and he and his mother are very obligated to us."

"How come?" Silver asked, her curiosity raised.

"He and his mother were very poor. Pipitza took his mother to be a teacher at the school where she was teaching, twenty-five or thirty years ago. She was very grateful to Pipitza. Because she was alone with Mimis then, with nobody to help them. Mimis loves his mother very much. He'll help you find a job.

"That'd be great."

"Mimi's mother told me you should go and visit Mimis at his office and talk to him. Maybe you can go there tomorrow afternoon. You take the bus from Platia Panipestimiou."

"About what time should I be there?"

"Five o'clock will be fine."

The atmosphere in Maria's living room was thick with love. Why Maria took such an interest in her wellbeing she could not figure out, as she was only a distant relative.

Chapter 27

The School

The classes started on October first. The school was called the Hellenic-American Institute in Athens, the place where the rich students learned English. Marula told her to enroll in the classes as English was increasingly becoming the language everyone was speaking all over Europe. One could find good employment in Athens if one knew English.

There was a test Silver had to take at the beginning of the school year so that they could determine at what level her English was.

The test was difficult. The written part was not bad, but the part where she had to recognize the spoken language and answer the questions correctly was more challenging.

Silver couldn't quite understand what the voice on the tape recorder said. She supposed it was the American English accent rather than the British English. Her teacher back in Romania was from England and her pronunciation was clear and slower. The recorded voice spoke different English. It was fast, the sounds were blended together, the words unfinished.

Silver knew she didn't do well on the test. First, the proctor explained what the test consisted of and what the rules were in

Greek, and Silver wasn't sure how much of the instructions she had understood.

They placed her near the beginner's level in a class where the teacher was a young American lady. The teacher was from New York and had become engaged to a Greek man and moved to Athens. She was of Greek heritage and also spoke Greek. The explanations were in Greek as all the other students in the class were Greek.

She started to study every morning at home for about four hours, completed all her homework, then left for a short visit to her uncle's shop and to buy whatever she needed for her dinner.

In the afternoon she attended classes. In the evenings she read English novels that she found at the second hand bookstores in Platia Panipestimiou. She couldn't learn fast enough. She practically devoured her books.

The weather changed and became cooler, with cold winds. Silver spent more and more time in her garsoniera, learning and reading.

Chapter 28

Mimis

Silver was dressed professionally, she thought. She took a copy of her diplomas with her just in case Mimis wanted to look at her credentials. It was hard to explain exactly what she had learned and done back in Romania, since she did not have a good command of the Greek language. She spoke in Greek, mimicking what she learned by listening to Maria and Teresa. She had never attended any classes in the Greek language; she didn't know how to read and write in Greek.

It was around 5 o'clock in the afternoon when Silver arrived at Mimis' office. She entered and asked to see him. Mimis came out of his office and invited her inside. A short man, he was stocky and in his forties. His gray hair was in great disarray as if he'd just awakened and had no time to comb it. His clothes were casual, his shoes well worn. Yet Silver knew from Maria that Mimis was now a rich man. He owned an engineering company and he owned real estate all over Greece.

"Hi, I'm Mimis." He extended his hand to Silver. "Maria told me you were going to stop by."

"I'm Silver. Pleased to meet you." Silver took his hand.

"Please, sit down and let me look at your papers. What kind of engineering were you engaged in back in Romania?"

"Civil engineering. I designed water treatment plants and water distribution and water tanks and reservoirs and pump stations back in Bucharest. I have a master's degree in civil engineering from the Hydrotechnical Institute in Bucharest."

"Impressive. But exactly what did you do, contacting engineering or consulting engineering?"

Silver was at a loss. She didn't know what contracting or consulting engineering meant. She worked in a huge engineering office located on the Calea Victoriei in Bucharest and she did design. That's what she knew. Contracting and consulting were new terms for her.

"We're a contacting engineering firm. That means we contract jobs to build, then to construct them."

"No, that's not what I did. I designed things, not constructed them."

"Then you couldn't work here with us, but I'll ask a friend of mine who we work with and has a consulting engineering company to talk to you. Maybe you can find a job with them. How is Maria? I have not seen her in a while."

"Maria is fine. She talks fondly about you and your mother."

"Yes. She and her sister Pipitza helped me and my mother to establish ourselves in Athens when we first came here from the islands. Please feel free to come and visit with us anytime. Check with me about every other day or at least once a week to see if I've found someplace for you to work."

"That's very kind of you. Maria told me that you are a busy man."

"That's O.K. Now that I think about it, I know the right man for you to marry to stay in Greece. Maybe next time you visit with us I'll introduce him to you."

"Really? That would be the best solution to all my problems." Silver said her hopes high again.

Silver knew she wanted to get married and have her own family and children. She wanted that even while in Romania, but it had not been meant to be. The man she fell for had married somebody else. Visiting Greece, her relatives, even her asking for political asylum was fine, she'd do whatever she had to do to help her family, but inside her heart she hoped for romance. She hoped to find love and to get married. True, she had fallen for George right from the beginning, but again that was not meant to be. From the last encounter at Nuly's house she has not seen or ever heard from George.

Since she left her cousins' house both Nuly and Marula had not come to visit her at her garsoniera or ask about her wellbeing. Silver went and visited with her mother's brother Take and his wife Vanghelitza, but neither Nuly nor Marula were ever around. Sometime Vanghelitza was watching Marula's children. They were all behaving as if her incident with Marula never happened, but Marula was avoiding her and Silver was avoiding Marula. Nuly, as his mother Vanghelitza related to Silver later, was upset with her for having to confront his friend George for her sake. As if it was all her fault. Nuly had said, "Did she really think to marry George? With his job? Did she really think she was up to it?" It was a comment that Silver found offensive. Sometimes going to the beaches by herself, Silver caught herself looking for George. It had been several months now that she had not heard anything from him. It was not meant to be.

That didn't mean that she gave up hope on finding love. Besides she was told by many that the easiest way of establishing herself in Greece was for her to marry. Then, after she had established herself in Greece she could try to bring her family over. Yes, marriage was a possibility she was considering. But not marriage without love. Only if she was to find the right man who would love her and she could love in return. She would not compromise herself for the benefit of staying in Greece or even for the benefit of helping her family. But she was open to Mimis' suggestion of finding the right man.

Chapter 29

Mr. Lavranos

Her request for political asylum in Greece hadn't advanced as quickly as Silver had thought it would. Silver returned to the police station alone, for questioning. It was a few months after her arrival and her Greek language had improved. Now she could talk for herself and answer the questions the police officer asked. Silver knew exactly what she wanted: to be allowed to stay and live and work in Greece and later, to be able to bring over her family from Romania. That had been her mother's utmost wish when she had sent Silver to Greece. Now it was Silver's utmost wish. In the few months she had been here, Silver had come to love Greece and Athens with the intensity that one loves her birth country. Greece had become her "patrida". Silver came to know Athens better than Bucharest, the place she had been raised in, and to love it even more.

Teresa introduced her to Mr. Lavranos, a lawyer, who promised to look after her papers at IPIA.

Nobody knew for sure what was going on inside the institution unless one had inside eyes and ears. That was the role of Mr. Lavranos.

Silver spent more than one afternoon in his office waiting for him to find a free moment and place a telephone call for her to the police station.

The answer was always the same. She must wait patiently.

Chapter 30

Costas

Silver climbed the stairs to Maria's apartment two at a time. Maria's voice sounded impatient when she opened the front door. Maria waited for her in the hallway.

"Hurry up and change and go to Mimis' office." Maria shouted as soon as Silver reached the hallway.

"Why? What happened?"

"I don't know. He called here and said for you to go to his office this afternoon. I was trying to reach you at Teresa's but you'd already left."

"What can it be?"

"I don't know. Maybe he found a job for you. Hurry up now and dress nicely."

"Thank you. I'm on my way."

Silver ran back to her apartment and changed quickly.

She decided to wear the Italian pants she just bought from the boutique. They were her only major expense of late. They were velvet gray and fit like a second skin on her slender body. On top, she put her Romanian sheer white blouse, soft like sea foam. She looked good with her face sun kissed, set off by the white blouse, as she inspected herself in the bathroom mirror.

It was around 6:30 p.m. when she reached Mimis' office. Everybody was preparing to go out for the evening. They were waiting for her and someone else to arrive.

Silver stood in Mimis' office next to the door when she saw from the corner of her eye, a young, tall, and elegantly dressed man entering the office. Did her heart skip a beat or was it just her overheated imagination? She was sure he was the man Mimis mentioned the other day that would make a good match for her. Otherwise why would Mimis have invited her over there? The gathering had nothing to do with finding a job for her.

"Finally you're here." Mimis said. "We were all waiting for you. This is Silver."

"Hi. I'm Costas. Mimis has told me so much about you." The stranger extended a long fingered hand toward Silver.

His English was fluent.

"Nice to meet you." Silver clasped his hand.

"We are all going to Buzuchea this evening. We're going to take three cars, so everybody find their places." Mimis directed.

Silver went in the car with Mimis' partner Nicos, a young man who specialized in machinery and equipment, and with Maria, the office's young secretary.

The famous restaurant, Buzuchea, was a vast place with tables set with white linen. There was dim candlelight and soft music played by a band in a corner of the huge room. In the center of the huge room was a fireplace, a jachea. Silver learned that the Greek custom was that after dinner, people threw their plates and glasses into the fireplace for good fortune.

Mimis ordered meals for the ladies, and drinks only for the men. They probably had a tacit understanding among them about the eating arrangements. Silver was seated between Costas and another man who worked for Mimis. On the other side of Costas sat Maria. Mimis was seated at the head of the long table. He was in charge.

The chanteuse sang soulful songs, one after the other. The wine was sweet, and Costas' presence softened Silver's heart.

How romantic. A young gypsy girl came near the table with fresh cut gardenias, their stems covered with silver foil, and offered them to the men to buy for the mistresses of their hearts.

Costas bought her a flower and Silver pinned it to her blouse. The sweet engulfing scent of the flower mixed with Costas' after-shave and the smell of the candles intoxicated Silver. She felt on dangerous ground, her common sense leaving her. Costas held out his hand and clasped Silver's hand into his. Silver felt like she was dreaming.

She rode back home with Costas.

"I understand you're an engineer. Mimis told me you're looking for a job."

"That's right."

"What are you doing all day since you're not working?" "I'm taking classes at the Hellenic-American

Institute."

"That's good. And what else?" "I'm going to the beaches."

"How do you get there without a car?"

"I've been taking the bus to wherever I want to go. Sometimes I'll stay all day to the beach. I take my books with me and study. What do you do?"

"I'm also an engineer. A safety engineer."

"Do you work for Mimis?"

"No. I'm working with a different company. Mimis is my friend. I'm helping him in the evenings with his safety papers. Do you have a phone I can reach you at?

"I don't. But you could call at Teresa's, my landlady.

She'll let me know."

"Would you like me to call upon you?"

"Yes. I'd like that." Again she did not like playing games. She certainly liked the man. Why not let him know it up front?

Chapter 31

Vasili

"So, what did Mr. Costas say today?" Teresa asked when Silver entered the living room from the hallway.

"He is studying for his master's thesis. He has an exam later this week."

"So, did he invite you somewhere later on this week?"

"Yes. He wants us to go to the beach this coming Sunday. I can't wait to see him."

"I'd say you're in love," Teresa added in an amused tone of voice. "And a bad case too."

She was seated at the dining table, a glass of Metaxa cognac in her hand. She sipped slowly enjoying the drink. "

"Where is Rania?" Silver asked.

"She's finishing her homework in her room."

"Teresa, you're drinking a lot. It is not good for you. Why are you doing this to yourself?"

"You don't know?" Teresa's speech was slurry, her eyes glossy, and her short, wavy hair was falling over her face.

"Vasili has left me for an other woman. And she had the audacity to call me here today."

"No, I didn't know." Silver answered, saddened.

"What happened?" Honestly, she knew the answer. Marula had told her about it from the beginning, and then Vangheli commented that if was not for the fact that Teresa's husband had left her, she would have never taken her in. According to Vangheli, the only reason Teresa took her in was because she felt alone and she needed a friend. That might have been true, and as sad it was for Teresa, Silver valued Teresa's friendship as a God sent gift.

"He went to Patra with his work and found another woman there. That's what happened."

"Why didn't you go with him? Why did you stay here in Athens instead of going with him to Patra?"

"Because of my mother. Who would take care of her if I left? And what about Rania and her school?"

"Rania could have gone to school in Patra." Silver offered.

"No, she's going to a private school for gifted children. I could not have done that to her."

"What about you? You lost your husband to another woman."

"That's why I am drinking. Now you know."

"You'll destroy yourself. And who'll take care of Rania and Yaya if something happens to you? You owe it to Rania, if not yourself, to stop drinking." Silver said.

"Have you ever been in love so much that you don't mind what's happening to yourself anymore? Do you know what love really is?"

"Yes, I do!"

"Have you been in love before?" Teresa asked.

"Yes, back in Romania."

"And what happened?"

"He married another woman after I waited for him for eight years." Silver answered. "Then it was my infatuation with George, here."

"So, you do know."

"Yes. But I didn't let it ruin my life. I moved on. It wasn't an easy task, I have to admit. It took me two years of mourning, back in Romania, but I am now back on my feet and looking for love again. Life goes on."

"Silver, I remember when I first saw you. You were with your cousin Marula. She was doing all the talking and you sat there. You know it was something in your eyes that made me accept you as my tenant. I saw right through Marula's lies. But it was a plea in your eyes that tugged at my heart."

Rania emerged from the other room, her homework in one hand, asking her mother how to spell a difficult word.

Chapter 32

Costas

"You said we were going to the beach." Silver said, adjusting her seat belt over her thick Romanian sheep skin coat. It was a white hand-embroidered coat that she wore with a big leather belt. Costas drove an old beat up car that was dark blue. It was getting dark outside and it was still cold.

"That's right. We're going to the beaches, you'll see." Costas answered. He was dressed as elegantly as ever, in a dark gray suit and a long gray overcoat.

"How was your exam? Did you pass it?"

"It wasn't an exam. I'm working on my master's thesis."

"Is it very hard to obtain your master's degree here? Do you have to study a lot?" Silver asked, as if she didn't know from her own experience how hard it was and how much study it took, as if she hadn't had to go through the same thing back in Romania while studying for her master's in engineering.

"It's a lot of work, of course. I have a regular job and then I go to school in the evenings and study for the exams."

"The guys who work for Mimis don't think so." Silver probed further. In reality what she heard at Mimis' office had disturbed her. Mimi's partner was talking with another guy at the office about how Costas wouldn't need to study so hard if he knew how to make money.

"Those who know about it can appreciate it. Your English is getting really good. I'm really proud of you. You must study hard yourself."

"Several hours a day." Silver answered.

They stopped in front of a small coffee shop outside Athens. They entered the deserted place and ordered pagoto- ice cream.

They walked to the seashore. The beach was high and rocky, not sandy. They climbed a high cliff hanging above the sea and sat down, close to each other. The weather was cold. It was mid February and the sky was dark. The sea foamed and beat against the rocks below their feet.

Silver didn't notice the cold. She leaned against Costas. His sensitive hands caressed her cheeks. Costas put an arm around her shoulders, pressing her close. His hand raised her chin slowly, and he kissed her deep on the mouth. How wonderful, Silver thought. Kissing Costas was like drinking water, fresh water from a well so refreshing that she could not drink enough to quench her thirst.

Maybe the guys at Mimis' office, including Mimis, thought Costas was not as smart as they were because he was not as rich as Mimis was, but she could appreciate his education and his sensitivity. She liked his studious nature. She was the same way. She loved books too. Who cared about Mimis' riches?

Chapter 33

Evghenia

"Mimis called yesterday. He has found a job for you. He wants you to be at his office tomorrow morning." Maria announced proudly as soon as Silver entered the living room. She was seated at the big table with Pipitza her sister, and Evghenia her niece, having coffee. Since Evgehnia had married last fall, Pipitza had come to live with Maria in the apartment. She left the house in Aghia Paraskevi to her daughter and her husband. Pipitza's other children Elias and George were already married and established in their own homes.

"Welcome and please sit down." Pipitza said in a kind voice. "We are always glad to see you. Would you like some coffee and couluretzi? Elias brought some fresh yesterday."

"Yes, thank you." Silver set down at the oval table. "What're you making, Pipitza? It looks like a tablecloth. How beautiful it is."

"Yes, it's a tablecloth. I'm crocheting one for Elias' wife since I've already made some for the other children. I can't just sit. My hands need to be doing something all the time. I can't remain still."

"So I noticed." Silver drank her strong Turkish coffee from the tiny finger cup. She watched Pipitza's hands. Big deft hard-working hands, slightly twisted by arthritis, with knobby knuckles. Silver shifted her gaze to Pipitza's face, full of wrinkles, with smiling eyes radiating love, the Godly love that came from within.

"Speaking of Mimis, did you know that when the children were young, Mimis' mother and I planned for Evghenia to marry Mimis?" Pipitza said.

"Is that so?"

"Yes. It never happened of course. Mimis went and married that ugly woman for her money. She is so ugly we call her 'the monster.'" Evghenia interjected. "Since he became rich he wants to divorce her, of course, but he's thinking of the girl. He has a young daughter, did you know?"

"I think I heard him talking about his daughter." Silver answered glancing at Evghenia. She was a big woman in her thirties, with a pretty face and light green eyes. Overweight, very overweight.

"That's one of them. He has another illegitimate daughter by his girlfriend. Did you meet his girlfriend?" Evghenia asked.

"I am not sure. There was, one time, a lady there I thought he was quite close to." Silver felt uncomfortable.

"Yes! She's the one! She lives near his office and visits him all the time there. She is married to a nice man too."

"I hope he found a good job for me." Silver said to change the subject. "I mean something I know how to do."

"You'll do just fine, I'm sure." Maria said in a kind voice. "Girls like you who work hard and mind their families are rare to find. How's Teresa doing?"

"Good. We have become close friends. I spend a lot of time upstairs talking to Teresa and Rania, especially now that is cold outside."

"How are your papers coming along? Any news from Mr. Lavranos?" Maria asked.

"Not yet. I'm very worried about it. Maybe now that I have a job they'll let me stay here." Silver added hopefully.

"I don't see why not. You were born here and your mother is Greek. They'll let you stay here." Maria said in a firm voice.

"We're all happy to have you here." Pipitza added.

Silver finished her coffee and left. She'd stop at her uncle's shop and talk to him for a while, then go back home to her garsoniera. She had to prepare for the next day if she was to start working.

Chapter 34

The Workplace

The next day at eight o'clock, Silver waited at the door of "Michael Zaharias and Daniel Sotiropulos- Hydravliki Engineers" - meaning hydraulics engineers. At least that's what the plaque at the entrance door to the building was announcing. Silver dressed professionally yet lightly since the weather had started to warm up.

Ten minutes after she arrived at the door, a man in his early forties with graying hair and a small potbelly approached.

"Hi, I'm Michael Zaharias." He shook her hand before he started searching his pockets for the keys to open the heavy entrance door to the multi-level building.

"I'm Silver, Mimis sent me. He said you need an engineer."

"Mimis told me you were coming today." He opened the front door. They climbed the stairs to the first floor where the engineering company was located. "Please, come into my office and let's talk a bit about your work experience and our needs. But first let me start the coffee."

"I studied in Romania and I'm a civil engineer. I was doing design."

"That's exactly what our company does, civil engineering design. Mimis probably told you that we have a project we're going to design that Mimis' company is going to construct. Actually, Mimis got the project and asked us to do the design work for him. Mimis is the one with all the right connections."

"Yes he mentioned something, but he did not explain the project."

"It's a water purification station for the island of Crete."

"That's in my line of experience. In Romania I designed water supply and resources, and water treatment and water purification plants. I finished the Hydrotechnical Construction Faculty."

"That's exactly what we specialize in, hydraulics. I was in the United States and worked there for a while at a company in Atlanta. That's where I got the idea about hydraulic engineering, and when I came back I opened a company here."

"Is that so? How did you like America? How are the people there? Are there jobs?"

"Personally I had a good job with an engineering company. I lived in a big house just outside of Atlanta, with a large yard. I even married an American woman, but I couldn't live there. I sold everything and brought my wife, back here."

"But why? What was wrong with America?"

"Nothing. Probably I was making more money than I'll ever make here. But Greece is my patrida. I couldn't live anywhere else. It's that simple. I had everything I could wish for and then some, but I wasn't happy." A young man entered the office. He was in his mid thirties, a bit overweight and with a receding hairline.

"Now tell her the truth, Michael! You couldn't live without Maria. That's the truth." He paused and peered directly at Silver. "Hi, I'm Dimitrios, the other half of the business."

"Hi, my name is Silver. Michael told me about the business. I'm ready to start work today. I have only one problem, I don't know how to write in Greek." Silver confessed.

"That's not important. You can do the calculations and design the plans and a draftsman can complete the writing part. All my books are in English. I brought them back with me from America." Michael added.

"That's good. I know English."

"Dimitrios is an assistant professor at the University, besides working here. The other employees are on a temporary basis, when we get work. After we're finished everybody is gone but Dimitrios and me. That's the only way we can survive."

"It's the same thing with my job?" Silver asked

"Yes of course. As soon as we finish the project everybody gets paid in accordance with the time he puts in on the job, and we close the office until the next job's lined up."

"What are the working hours?"

"We work from eight o'clock in the morning to noon and then take a siesta for lunch. We come back to work at four o'clock in the afternoon and work until maybe six or eight at night, or as long as we need to. If you want to make a lot of money you can work longer hours." Michael informed her.

For the next three weeks the place looked like a bees' nest. People came in and out, doing their work. Draftsmen and clerical staff were hired as well as a secretary. They all appeared to know what they were doing. Probably they'd been a part of the team for a long while.

Silver and Michael and Dimitios designed the plans and made the engineering computations. The draftsmen drafted the plans, and the clerks made prints and put the set of drawings together. The secretary typed the specifications for the project.

The business worked like well-oiled machinery. Everybody was efficient and knew their part in the big scheme of preparing a project.

Both Michael and Dimitrios were very good engineers. Silver worked well with the two of them. She understood and was familiar with the design of the project.

Silver put in as much time as she physically could until they finished the project. She got paid 17,000.00 drachmas, in hand. The equivalent of three month's rent and utility expenses. Not bad.

Chapter 35

Costas

"This time we're going to the beaches." Costas glanced over at Silver as she sat in the seat next to him, in his old, dark blue car.

The weather was warming up again, and the beach season had begun.

Silver didn't recognize the route. It was not the "Leuforou Vasileus" she traveled with George, last summer.

When they arrived, it was a different site completely.

There was a small tavern on the shore where they stopped for lunch. Tables were arranged outside under a cluster of trees in the shade, covered with red-and-white checkered tablecloths. Costas ordered fish-and-chips, and they ate sitting close to each other, happy to be together.

They went to the beach and stretched out in the sun. Silver could not coax herself to enter the water yet, it was too cold, but Costas ventured into the sea and swam for a while. When he came back on the shore water glistened on his lean, powerful body.

He lay back on the towel next to Silver, and she put her head on his chest. The mat of curly, dark hair seemed pleasantly wet and cold, refreshing to her heated cheek.

Later when they returned to the car, someone had left a massage on Costas' beeper.

"It was my father." Costas said, sounding anxious. "I have to go back to the beach and call home right away. Maybe somebody needs me."

They went to the tavern and Costas talked to his father while Silver waited at a distance. She didn't want to intrude.

"There are some clients of mine waiting at home to talk to me. I have to rush back." Costas explained.

He hurried now, as if what he was doing with Silver at the beach was forbidden, a stolen moment. As if he had to go back to his duty, to something important. His job and the needs of his family. It was as if Silver was no longer important. Silver understood, but in the bottom of her heart she felt shut out. As if his parents, his home, and his work were off limits to her. She was not part of it.

She knew Costas put a lot of time into his work and his studying but he seldom discussed it with her. Costas had not taken her to meet his family yet.

He was keeping her at a distance. There were things they had not discussed openly, such as his intentions toward her. What if she was not allowed to remain in Greece? What about their romance then? Was he seing other girls as well? Was he serious about her? Did he love her? They behaved as lovers but he had not mentioned anything about love. Even his relationship with Mimis remained a mystery to her. Costas seemed sincere in his admiration for Mimis. She had never heard a bad word from Costas about Mimis, or anybody else in the office for that matter.

Those thoughts were constantly in her mind. Yet she could not bring herself to ask Costas directly. She was too shy and too proud.

That stupid pride of hers again, or maybe it was just plain coward-ice. Her feelings toward him were deepening with each encounter. What about his feelings toward her? She was taught that the man should be the first to talk about such things. It was shameful for a woman to open the discussion on such matters of the heart, and proclaim her feelings openly before the man did so. No, not really shameful, but it was a game of waiting for the other person to say it first. As if she said it first she would lose. She would lose Costas' love and respect.

He dropped her at her apartment, kissed her hurriedly on the cheek, and went on to his affairs.

She tried not to let her disappointment show.

Chapter 36

Maria

Silver knew that the issues with her papers at IPIA, her request for political asylum in Greece, would soon to come to a head when Maria appeared that night at her apartment door.

It was near midnight when a sharp knock woke Silver. She opened the door to Teresa and Maria standing in the hallway outside her apartment. Silver could see Maria was agitated, her long white hair usually so neatly arranged in a bun at the nape of her neck hung down her shoulders in disarray.

Silver invited them inside her bedroom/living room, dressed only in her nightgown, her bed unmade.

"I cannot put my name down to guarantee you to stay here. I thought I could, but my nephew told me not to do so, as I could damage his career. He's with the Diplomatic Corps and you coming from a Communist country, it's a delicate issue. I am so sorry." Maria talked so quickly Silver could hardly understand.

"Who asked you to guarantee me?" Silver asked, trying hard to comprehend.

"Mr. Lavranos called Teresa this evening, and Teresa called me and asked if I would guarantee you to stay here, as your other relatives refused to do so." Maria responded. "At first I said that I would, because I love you so much and I want you to stay here, but my nephew told me no to do it. I am so sorry."

"So, that what it is." Silver was very hurt. Her own relatives would not guarantee her. They were afraid that they might have to support her monetarily in case she couldn't make it on her own.

"I'm not able to do it either," Teresa interjected "as I am not your relative."

"I understand, and I thank you both for trying so hard to help me stay here." Silver's heart was heavy. Who was to help her if her own relatives turned their back on her? "So what's going to happened next?"

"Mr. Lavranos told us that they would have you called in front of a committee to ask you questions, an Epitropi, and they would decide what to do with you then. It's scheduled for the day after tomorrow, he said."

"So that's how it is." Silver's heart was heavy and she was worried.

What was going to happen to her and her family? Their lives were hanging on what the Epitropi would decide for her.

Teresa and Maria left, and Silver went back to bed. She tried to think, sleep totally forgotten.

Stories came down from "Latrium" the immigrant's camps located just outside Athens. Her uncle Vangheli, in that his shop was centrally located and because he spoke some Romanian, talked with the Romanian refugees from the camps. They stopped by his shop sometime on Sunday afternoons when they had a free pass from the camps and when Vangheli had time to talk to them. They were people like herself who defected from Romania, and were on their way to United States, Canada or Australia. Places in the world where they received immigrants. They first had to stay six months in a transition country like Greece, Austria, or Italy. There, their papers were carefully checked and a "sponsor" was tracked down for them in the country where they wanted to move.

It was well known that the hardest place to be accepted as an immigrant was the United States. The standards were high for America.

Those people who had their lives on hold for at least six months tried to survive in Athens. The camps provided food and shelter, but horrid stories made their way down to her uncle's shop.

Single women like her, or women who were married but waiting for their husbands and families, were raped systematically by men of different origins and social status, living in the camps.

The Greek police did not intervene there.

The law of the "strongest" governed the camps. There were stories of women who chose to end their lives rather than continue being raped night after night.

There were refugees from all corners of the world, waiting to be received by various countries.

Silver had heard all of that, and considered herself fortunate, very fortunate indeed. She knew she wouldn't have survived if she had had to stay in the camps, alone.

What was going to happen to her now? God watched over her, she felt sure.

Chapter 37

"The Epitropi"

"Mother. It's me, Silver. Everything is over." Silver shouted in the phone, watching the yellow light filtering through the stained glass panels of the closed French doors in Teresa's foyer.

"What is over? Start at the beginning. What's going on?" Mother sounded as through she was next door.

"I went to the Epitropi this morning and they decided that I can't stay here."

"Why not? Tell me exactly what happened from the beginning." Mother said, her voice anxious and full of worry.

"This morning I came before the committee at IPIA. They asked me a lot of questions, and they told me they can't help me bring my family over."

"From the beginning again. What did they ask you?"

"Who I am, what education I have, what languages do I speak, what do I know to do to survive here. All that was O.K.! They also mentioned that if I would get married here I would be allowed to stay."

"That would have been the best of all. Did Costas ever mention anything like that to you?"

"Of course not. Otherwise you would be the first to know."

"So what did they not like about you?"

"I told them that I expected them to help you all come here."

"That was stupid. Why did you have to complicate things now?"

"I had to know. We cannot stay separated for a lifetime. Better to know up front."

"That would have come later, after you had a chance to establish yourself there. Once you had gotten a permanent job, and had some income of your own. Now what is going to happen?"

"I don't know. That's why I called. What do you all want to do? I could either come back home to Romania, or go to America, Australia or Canada. That's where they receive refugees."

"If you go to America, would we be able to come there too?"

"I think so. That's what they told me today. I asked the question."

"This is a very hard decision to make. I think we have a cousin in America, in New York. One of my mother's sisters, Thana, married in America some time ago. She had three sons there. I could find the address of one of her sons. I'll send it to you! Let me talk to Teresa for a minute to thank her for taking care of you and taking you into her house."

Silver handed the phone to Teresa and heard Teresa and her mother chatting quickly in Greek.

She would go forward to America. It was decided. There were a lot of things she had to do now.

She heard from the other Romanian refugees she had met at Vangheli's shop that she had to sign up with a society like the Red Cross or World Churches Services to request their help to emigrate to America. She would have to pass an interview with the American Embassy in Athens. She would have to pass the physical examination, and she would have to find somebody to "sponsor" her in America.

Not an easy task.

In a way she was at peace, at last. She had done everything in her power to stay in Greece. She had tried so hard. Now, there were only two routes from there. Unless of course, she was to get married. She could go back to Romania and go on with her life there as if nothing happened, as if she had returned from an extended vacation in Greece. But she knew. Her and her family's future would be finished. They would not be allowed to travel any longer. Maybe she would not have a job. Maybe there would be repercussions for the family.

Or, she could go forward to America to whatever life there had to offer. She'd take the latter. She was not a coward. She did not like the feeling of being defeated. Mother was the same way.

Chapter 38

Alexander

Her hair was growing long and dull, with dark roots. Silver did not like it any longer. When she had arrived in Athens, after Marula returned from vacation, Silver went with her to a parlor. Marula knew all the free places and took advantage of them. She used to go to a place, a Beauticians' School, where students were learning how to do hair. Marula had thick naturally curly hair that resisted all treatments the students exposed her hair to. To be fair, Marula's hair always looked good and fashionable. It was her greatest asset. She changed her hair color quite often, but that was part of her charm.

Silver's hair was fine. That first time, when she went with Marula, she let the students dye her hair red. But now her hair had started to grow, and despite her best efforts to set it on big rolls, it was limp. Time for a total hair change, she decided.

Maria's niece, the American who married her nephew, use to do her hair at "Alexander's." It was the most expensive and exclusive salon in all of Athens.

Silver got some money from her engineering job, and decided to treat herself to the best. She would go to "Alexander's" and have her hair done.

She asked Maria's niece to make an appointment for her. She would have her hair cut. That's all, she decided before hand. How much could a hair cut cost? Even at the most expensive places, that couldn't be too expensive. If the haircut was good, she could arrange her hair easily afterwards.

When she arrived, the assistant asked her very courteously about her relatives that recommended the salon to her, Maria's nieces. Silver understood from the reverence of the hairdressers that Maria's nieces were well to do.

They shampooed her hair, analyzed it, talked amongst themselves about it, then gave her a permanent without even consulting her, doing what they thought would be best for her looks.

These people thought that she was as rich as Maria's nieces were. Who knew how much a permanent cost? She couldn't turn back and leave, or say she had money only for a haircut. This was a place for the wealthy. She was sure nobody discussed prices, only hair fashion and how to improve one's looks. She started to feel nervous. "What would come next?"

They washed her perm so the curl didn't set too tightly. Alexander himself came and cut her freshly permed hair to the latest fashion. Watching Alexander's hands as they artfully cut her hair, and the way her face changed after the hair cut, Silver forgot about the cost and the money. He was an artist doing his job.

After Alexander finished with the cut, helpers curled her hair. When they were through with her she looked like a different person, as if she were a model stepping out from a hair catalog.

Finally she had to pay the bill. It amounted to half of her monthly expenses, including the rent.

It was worth it, every penny.

Chapter 39

Mother

"Mother, did you talk to father and Mady and Radu? What have they decided about me going to America?" Silver was once again in Teresa's foyer calling home. She had arranged with Teresa to allow her to call her mother from her telephone and to add the expenses to her monthly rent. It was more convenient and safe for her to call from Teresa's than from the public telephones in Omonia.

"Yes, we talked, and we decided, all of us, that you should go forward to America only if you make sure we can follow later."

"I've checked. Once I'm an American citizen, five years after my arrival in America, I'll have the right to ask for my family to be reunited with me."

"That's good! We're all behind you."

"Mother, I need you to send me my original engineering diploma and the transcripts from the college. I'll need those when I go. Also, please send my duvet. In New York it will be cold during the winters. Did you find the address of your cousin in New York?"

"I'll write it to you in my next letter. Listen, I've met a Greek Doctor who is visiting with his relatives here, Dr. Barzas. He'll bring your diploma. I've already talked to him. He also said that his cousins are there at the refugee camp in Greece, waiting to go to Canada. See if you can locate them and get some advice from them. They're a serious family. I think Dr. Barzas mentioned the man is an engineer also."

"I'll try to find them. Is Dr. Barzas going to call me when he's back in Greece?"

"Yes, I gave him Vangheli's telephone number at the shop. He'll find you!"

"It looks like you're all set to go to America." Teresa came from the living room as soon as Silver hung up the phone.

"Yes, it looks that way."

"Do you know how long you'll be here before leaving?" "I have no idea. I have to go and sign with one of those societies that help refugees to go to America. Red Cross or the World Church Services. I'll know more after that. Several months, I'd say."

"So you'll not be here next year. I'll have to rent the garsoniera downstairs, your garsoniera, for the next

year. Students usually rent the garsonieras, and they start the school year in September. I have to rent it by August. You do understand? That's my only source of income since Vasili left, that and the tutoring."

"Yes, of course I understand."

"I'll move you upstairs into the garsoniera on the fourth floor, off the terrace."

"That'll be perfect Teresa, don't worry about me."

So, she would have to move upstairs into the smaller garsoniera. She also had to start thinking about packing her belongings for the big trip in America. A lot of things to take care of.

Chapter 40

Acropolis

"What did you do to your hair?" Costas sounded surprised.

"I've cut my hair. Do you like it?"

"I don't know. I liked it better the way you had it before, longer and the lighter color too. It looked soft and feminine."

"You mean you don't like it now? After I spent a fortune on it? I went to "Alexander's" to have it done."

"I don't know. I liked it better long, it was more feminine."

Silver met Costas in the park at the toe of Acropolis.

He promised to show her the Acropolis and the historic museum. She'd walked to the park and met Costas there. It was noon, and Costas had taken the afternoon off from his job to go with her. He was waiting for her in the park in the shadows of the trees. First, when she got there, she hadn't seen him and thought he might have not arrived yet. Then after a few minutes of her looking around he had made his appearance from under the trees' shade.

The thought of him hiding from the onlookers and potential acquaintances came to Silver's forefront. It was just an annoying feeling. As if he didn't want to be seen with her. A strange feeling she could not put her finger on. Then, maybe it was only her imagination.

They started to climb the many flights of white marble stairs to the Acropolis. Silver wished she hadn't worn

high-heeled sandals. Her feet ached already.

When they arrived at the temple, Silver admired the statues of young women, the virgins, holding the temple's beams over their heads.

"They are imitations made of synthetic resins, you know." Costas offered. "The real ones are already inside, preserved."

"Why is that?"

"The smog here in Athens is very bad and an international committee of specialists was formed to preserve the temple. They decided to move the original statues inside, in order to protect them."

"Should we go inside and visit the museum?"

They went inside the museum and visited room after room of artifacts and statues. Costas explained to her the history and the meaning behind each statue and the mythology behind them. He was so knowledgeable. Silver's heart started to sink in her chest. There was so much pride and love in Costa's eyes and his voice.

They moved slowly from one piece to the next Costas explaining the history behind everything they saw. His eyes sparkled, as Silver had never seen before. He would never leave Greece. For all his English education and his sophistication Costas was first a Greek. He loved his country. He would never leave it and follow her to America, regardless of what he might say. Her mind was not on the historic pieces they were seeing. She was trying to figure out what Costas was thinking, what his reaction would be to the news of her imminent departure. Did he even care? What were his feelings and intentions toward her? She'd just have to tell him the facts and try to understand his reaction.

"I have to go to America. They will not let me stay here in Greece."

"Is that so. When do you have to leave?"

"As soon as they find me a "sponsor" in the United States. My mother sent me the address of one of her cousin's, a teacher, who lives in New York. I'll write to him to ask if he would be willing to sponsor me."

"That sounds like a good plan." Costas said.

She could not figure anything out from the tone of his voice. He acted as if her departure didn't affect him. Was that all there was to their relationship?

"My high heeled sandals are killing my feet."

"We'll going back now. If you want I can carry you to my car."

"Thank you, but I think I can manage."

Silver's feelings were hurt by his apparent lack of interest in her departure. Men were certainly totally different creatures. How could she find out what he really felt or what he really thought? He didn't offer any insights about his feelings. She would have to talk to somebody about him, probably Maria.

Chapter 41

The Barzas Family

Silver asked the other Romanians she knew where the Barzas family lived. They told her that they lived in a dilapidated hotel, close to Platia Omonia, along with other refugee families. The World Church Service had housed them there.

Silver went to visit them. She found the hotel and the Barzas family in a room on the second floor of the hotel. She knocked on the door and a man in his early forties opened it. The room was quite big and had four metal beds, all of them unmade and without bed spreads, crammed one next to the other, occupying the entire space. In a corner were a small lavatory and a portable gas stove on top of a cabinet.

A woman in her mid-forties and two teen-age boys were also in the room.

"My name is Silver Costin. My Mother told me about Dr. Barzas, whom she met in Bucharest, and Dr. Barzas mentioned you all." It had been a while since she had spoken Romanian to anybody besides her mother.

"I'm Nicu Barzas and this is my wife Anna and our children."

"I heard you're waiting to go to Canada?"

"No, we're waiting to be approved for the United States. We have relatives in New Jersey."

"Which organization did you sign up with?"

"The World Churches Services," the man answered.

"There is a Romanian lady there who helped us. She'll help you too."

"And how exactly did she help you?" Silver asked.

"First, she put us here, instead of sending us to "Latrium", outside Athens. They give us the room and utilities for free. There is a common bathroom at the end of the hallway we can use. And they give us 100 drachmas per day per person." the man mentioned.

"Enough for the four of us to buy food that I cook here on the stove. Maybe we have enough money left over at the end of the day to buy a stamp to write back home. We don't need anything else. We are content." the woman said. She was a heavy woman with short brown hair. She wore blue sweat pants and a light blue sleeveless blouse. Her face was prematurely lined.

"I heard that in the camps outside Athens it's a lot worse." Silver said.

"Of course. There you are not free to leave and come to Athens. You need a pass. We were lucky to find the Romanian lady at the World Churches organization. We're a family, that's why they kept us here, but also my wife knows how to sew and she made several dresses for this lady at the organization."

"So, that's how is done." Silver commented more to her self. "I'm very lucky I have relatives from my mother's side here in Athens."

"So we heard. What are going to do now? Will they let you stay here?" the man asked.

"No. I have to apply, like you did, to one of those organizations to allow me to go to the Unites States. How long have you been here?"

"About four months and we're lucky. We already have a sponsor, our relatives in New Jersey. Our cousins in New Jersey have rented a house for us next to theirs. They are waiting for us. Other people are waiting from six months to one year and a half."

"What exactly these organizations are doing for you?"

"They keep you for as long as you need to clear your papers and be approved by one of the countries that receives refugees. They arrange an interview with the respective Embassy, they offer English classes, and they will give us the air plane tickets to go to the United States."

"That's quite a bit," Silver said. "I heard that both of you are engineers. I am an engineer also. What has your cousin in America told you about finding jobs there? Is it easy to find a job as an engineer?"

"We go to New Jersey. That's a highly industrial area. I'm convinced I'll find something."

"Where do I go to apply to go to the United States through the same organization you are being helped by?"

"If you come here tomorrow morning at eight o'clock, I'll take you myself." the man offered.

"That'd be so nice. Thanks and good luck to you all." Silver was ready to go. Her mind worked quickly trying to figure out what her next step should be.

She and the Barzas family had spent about the same amount of time in Greece. How different their experiences had been. Those people knew where they were going and how they were going to get there. They stayed in the camps, they spent a minimum amount of money, and they learned English. They were preparing to go to America. That was their goal. Athens and Greece was a transitional point on their map. Nothing to be concerned with. They were living among Romanians and other refugees at the camps and they did not even consider learning anything about Greece, its people, its customs.

How different her time spent in Greece had been. All her heart, all her emotions were tightly interwoven with Greece and Athens.

It was her place of birth. Her blood was speaking louder than her mind. She loved the city. She loved the people. She wanted to stay there and would have given anything to do so. She would have spared no amount of patience and energy if she thought there might be a chance for her to stay. But facts are facts and after the Epitropi she knew for a fact that she could not stay.

Chapter 42

Maria

Silver visited with Maria that afternoon. Pipitza was out. She played cards once a week with her friends. Maria's neighbor from across the hallway, Mrs. Papadopoulos, was visiting with her. She was an old lady, about the same age as Maria. They got together a few times a week in the afternoons and had coffee and coulouretzs and chatted.

That afternoon Silver visited with a specific goal in her mind. She had spoken with Maria beforehand about Costas and the fact that she couldn't understand what he felt about her and her imminent departure. Did he care at all?

Maria suggested she ask him to pick her up that afternoon from her house so that Maria would have a chance to meet and judge him for herself. In Greece, even in these times, parents sometimes prearranged marriages. It was in some cases, if not in most cases, a transaction as the bride needed to have "prika", or dowry, in order to be married. But on the other hand marriages from love were also common. Silver thought that in the absence of her mother, Maria could ask some direct questions on her behalf.

"Do you speak French?" Ms. Papadopoulos said. "Maria told me you speak French and I would like to exercise my French."

"I studied French throughout school, but I don't know how fluent my French is after so many years." Silver said.

"Maria told me you speak French, otherwise I would not have come today." the older women said stubbornly.

"Did you see Costas?" Maria asked.

"I've talked to him and asked him to come and pick me up from here, if that's all right with you."

"Of course. I told you to bring him over, so I could see him and judge for myself."

"He'll be here any moment now to pick me up."

"I'd like to see him too." Ms. Papadopoulos said. "My husband died ten years ago but I still remember how good it was to have a man to put your head next to on the pillow at night. You know you have to be nice to him when he comes home from work. Like I was with my husband. He would come home tired from his job and I would ask him about his day and he would take me in his lap and talk to me. I'd listen and caress his hair and prepare his food and serve him at the table."

"But I'm working. I've a difficult job, as an engineer." Silver answered a bit annoyed with the old lady. "Things have changed. Women work too."

"I was working." the old lady said. "And I'm educated. I speak several languages. But the trick is to let your man feel he is smarter, more important, that he's the breadwinner in the house. You might have a job but the man's job is more important."

Silver listened, but her mind was not on the conversation.

A knock came at the door and Silver went to let Costas inside. He looked as elegant as ever in his gray suit, tall and handsome.

"Costas, this is Maria, my cousin, and Ms. Papadopoulos. This is my friend, Costas." Silver made the introduction as she ushered Costas inside.

"Good afternoon. I came to pick up Silver. We're going for a ride."

"So nice to met you, finally." Maria said. "Silver has told me so much about you. Please sit down and have some coffee and coulouretzs."

"Thank you, but I can't stay long." Costas said. "We're going for only a short ride. I have to go back home early this evening. I have a paper to prepare."

"Silver mentioned that you're preparing for your master's degree. How nice. But please do sit for few minutes, until Silver is ready." Maria insisted.

"Thank you." Reluctantly Costas took a place at the table.

"How's Mimis? It has been awhile since I've seen him."

"The same, I suppose. Mimis doesn't change."

"Where do you live?" Maria asked.

"In Aghia Paraskevi. I'm living with my family. I have my own apartment, but in their house."

"That's very nice. Before you came we're just discussing love."

Silver sat at the square table sipping her coffee and absently nibbling on a coulouretz. Her heart was beating fast, choking her. Maria was bold. She grilled him.

"Oh!"

"Yes, we were talking how hard is for two people to find each other these days. It is a once in a life time event, a chance two people have to connect, and if they don't take it when it presents itself, if they don't recognize for what it is, then the chance, the moment, can pass them by and be lost in space. What a pity that is, don't you think?"

Silver felt her face flushing violently. She could not believe her ears. Maria actually said it!

"Yes, I suppose so," Costas said in guarded tone.

"We know Silver and her family from back in Romania. We know her mother, and we love Silver very much. We think she's a very good girl. You don't find somebody like that every day, do you?"

"Silver told me that you and your sister, Pipitza, have been very good to her. I think it's time we left. Are you ready?" Costas turned to Silver.

"Yes, of course." Silver said. "Maria, I'll talk to you tomorrow. Good night Mrs. Papadopoulos."

"Good night. Have a nice ride. Come back and see me."

"I will, good night."

They left Maria's house and went to the car Costas had parked outside.

Silver felt embarrassed by Maria's direct approach. She never gave her permission to be so direct. But in all fairness, Maria told Costas what needed to be said, and quite nicely. Maria had a poet's heart.

"I received a letter from my uncle in New York," Silver said.

"What did he say?"

"That he's glad I got in touch, that he knew his mother had three sisters in Greece. He's a teacher at a high school near New York. He's not married."

"Did he assure you he's going to sponsor you?

"No, he didn't say that. He mainly talked about himself and the hard time he has with the students in the New York's school system these days."

"I'll drop you off now. As I told you, I have to be home early this evening."

"That's perfectly all right with me. Thank you for the ride."

He did not kiss her good night.

Silver went upstairs to her garsoniera. She had mixed feelings about the evening. She still didn't know what to make of Costas' behavior. He had not referred directly to Maria' s comments. She would ask Maria tomorrow for her reaction.

✧ ❖ ✧

Chapter 43

Maria

The next day Silver stopped by Maria's. "What did you think of him?" Silver asked as soon as she entered the living room.

"He's handsome, that's for sure!"

"I know that, but what did you think about his behavior toward me?"

"He's very slick. He did not say anything back to me. Did you like my comment about the two of you being lost in space if he doesn't make his move in time?"

"First I was embarrassed. I thought it was somewhat direct. But after I thought for a while, I decided it was all right."

"He did not answer anything. I don't know what to make of him. Did he say anything to you on your ride?" Maria asked.

"No. He didn't bring up the subject."

"We, Pipitza and I, are going to Vuliagmeni next week. We're going to rent an apartment for the summer. We do that every year. Then the family, the children, visit with us every weekend. You're welcome to visit with us any time." Maria offered.

"I'd like that. Maybe I'll came over next weekend." Silver said, and got ready to leave. She had a lot of things to take care of now. She had to go to the World Churches Organization with Nicu to fill out the application to emigrate to America. She had no more time for idle thoughts and wishes.

Chapter 44

The World Churches Services

At eight o'clock that morning, Silver was waiting for Nicu outside the hotel where the Barzas family lived. They were going to the World Churches Services. Nicu came out and they both walked to the Organization's headquarters. Nicu was a tall man, slender in his blue jeans and light blue shirt with short sleeves.

"I'll introduce you to the Romanian lady who helped us." Nicu ushered her through a huge open room crowded with people. They stopped at a desk covered with papers. A small woman in her mid-forties greeted them in Romanian.

"Hi Nicu, how is everybody in your family?"

"We're all fine, thank you. I've brought another Romanian girl, Silver, who wants to emigrate to America."

"Hi. How are you? I'm Helene." the small lady extended her hand toward Silver.

"I'm an engineer from Romania. I want to go to the United States."

"I have to go to English class." Nicu excused himself and departed, leaving the two of them alone.

"Goodbye Nicu, say hello from me to your family."

"First you have to complete the forms, and then we will let you know when you are scheduled for an interview with the American Embassy." Helene explained in a soft voice.

"I'll fill out the papers now, if you will allow me." Silver said. Suddenly she was anxious to go ahead with the plan to go to the United States.

"Sure. It's crowded here, but we can find you a place to fill out the application. If you are approved by the Embassy, you'll have to pass a complete physical examination before to go to America. Did anybody tell you that it would be difficult to be approved by the American Embassy? They're very picky as to whom they receive in United States. But since you're an engineer, you have a better chance."

The older woman talked to her quickly in Romanian, as if sharing secrets.

"How long have you been here in Athens?"

"For about eight months now. I tried to stay here because I have relatives from my mother' side, but they would not help me."

"Where do you live now?"

"I rent a garsoniera."

"Who pays for the rent and the utilities?"

"I do. My mother sends me things and I sell them and pay the rent. I also worked for a short while. I spend very little money."

"I see. If you want, we can help you with the rent until you leave for America. How much is your rent?"

"5,000 drachmas a months."

"We will give you $4,000 a month. That's what we gave everybody else, regardless to where they live. Did Nicu tell you that the organization is going to provide you with the airplane ticket once you are approved by the American Embassy and you find yourself a sponsor?"

"What's the story with the "sponsor"? Do I have to find myself a sponsor in America or is the Organization going to find somebody for me?"

"If you want to leave quickly, you must find your own sponsor. Maybe you have a relative over there?"

"Yes, my mother gave me the address of her cousin in New York. I contacted him and asked him to sponsor me."

"That's good. Otherwise the organization would find a church to sponsor you, but you never know how that will turn out."

"There are, I suppose, a lot of people applying everyday and going to America or other places?"

"There are a lot of people, like you said, and let me tell you something, there will be times when you'll regret the decision to leave Romania. Things are not easy over there either. You have to work hard to make it. It depends. I hear back from people who regret leaving, who have a hard time accommodating and adjusting to the new life. Others are doing well. I think it all depends on the attitude of the person. I remember a few years ago, there were three young men in their late twenties, two engineers and an architect from Romania. They went to Toronto, Canada. They still write to me from there. They're doing wonderfully. They adjusted well. They found jobs, and they're happy. It all depends! Here, fill out these applications and when you're ready, return them to my desk."

Silver sat down where Helene directed her, and started filling out the applications. She'd have to talk to Dr. Barzas also. Mother had sent her engineering diploma through him. Mother told her that Dr. Barzas had a son in New York.

It had been hard to make the decision to leave for America. Once that was decided she felt better, relieved. She had a plan to follow and a future to look forward to.

◄ ❖ ❖ ❖ ►

Chapter 45

Dr. Barzas

Dr. Barzas waited for her at her uncle Vangheli's shop. When Silver entered the dark shop, blinded for a moment from the outside light, she saw a small funny looking older man sitting on the spare chair by the display window. He held a briefcase tightly on his lap.

"Silver, this is Dr. Barzas." Vangheli made the introduction. "Your mother sent him here."

"Mother told me about you. Did you bring my diploma with you?" Silver spoke in Romanian.

"Yes, I did. It was very hard, you know, to sneak it past the customs in Romania." the small man said in fluent Romanian.

"Yes, I know. That's why I did not take it with me when I left. But then, I said I was going to visit with my relatives here. No need for the diploma then. How are mother and the rest of my family? Did you visit them?"

"They're all fine and they send you their love."

Dr. Barzas opened his briefcase with caution and took out her diploma, badly wrinkled.

"What happened to my diploma? Why is so wrinkled?

"I had to sneak it beneath my shirt. I couldn't risk anybody finding it in my luggage. You know they search the luggage at the custom point in Romania."

"Of course. Thanks a lot for taking it with you. You took a tremendous risk to bring it over."

"I'm now a Greek citizen. They wouldn't do anything to me, but I couldn't take the risk of them finding your diploma and confiscating it at the custom point. I know you'll need it in America."

"How nice of you."

"I have a son who is a doctor and lives now in New York."

"My mother told me about him."

"He went to study medicine in Barcelona, Spain as an exchange student and went directly from there to America after he finished the school. He married a Romanian girl he met in Barcelona and they both left for America."

"What about you and your wife?"

"We defected from Romania to Greece since I was born here, of Greek parents."

"Why didn't you go to America to be with your son?"

"We went and visited with two times now. His wife doesn't like us. You'll be happy that you made the decision to go to America. That's where your future is. Here there's nothing for you. It's very hard to learn the Greek language with the different alphabet and all."

"But you got your degree recognized here. You're a doctor here, what's so bad about it?"

"I still have difficulty with the Greek language. If you're a professional you have to be at that level regardless of where you came from."

"Isn't it true in America also?"

"Yes, but the English language is easier to learn for us. It has a Latin root, like Romanian, and has the phonetic alphabet."

"I suppose you're right about that. But here I'm closer to my family in Romania."

"You'll be closer to your family from America than from here. They have a Romanian community. They get together for special occasions and have Romanian food and songs and dances. The American government will help you bring over your family from Romania."

"That's good to know."

"Come and visit with me and my wife one day." "Thanks a lot. I will." Silver promised.

She liked Dr. Barzas. He was a courageous man to have taken her diploma with him. He looked nice and sad at the same time. He probably missed his son tremendously.

Chapter 46

Vula

Silver planned to spend that weekend with Maria and Pipitza, at Vuliagmeni. She had formed the habit of going almost daily to the beaches. The weather was warm and she took the bus from Platia Panipestimiou and went every day to a different beach site on the coast. She went to Vula and Vuliagmeni, to Gliffada and Sonio. The bus ride itself was a beautiful adventure, with the road high on the coast, meandering next to the seashore. She took a novel with her, and her lunch box, and spent the better part of the day lying in the sun and swimming. Her body became fit and strong, tanned from the sun, and lean. She was accumulating the sun's energy for the coming year, for the upcoming trip into the unknown.

Saturday morning, Silver took the bus and went to Vuliagmeni to visit with Maria. The bus ride was about two hours. She arrived there by ten o'clock. The apartment Maria and Pipitza rented was in an old building located one block from the beach. It was on the second floor of the building, and had a wide balcony. It had two bedrooms, a small kitchen, and a bathroom. On weekends Pipitza's children and their wives and children visited. On Sundays the entire family sat down together for dinner. On Saturdays it was not so crowded. Silver preferred to go on Saturday and not interfere with the family's gathering.

When she arrived, Vula, Pipitza's daughter-in-law and her child were there. Vula was an American girl, tall, blond, and beautiful. Pipitza's youngest son, George, was in the Navy and when he was stationed in Houston, Texas a few years back, he had met Vula and married her. Now he was still in the Navy but worked out of the headquarters in Athens. He was the only one of Pipitza's three children who had a child. The entire family's love and attention centered on the little boy. Vula was American, but of Greek heritage. She spoke both English and Greek.

Vula was seated at the table on the veranda with little George on her lap when Silver arrived. Maria and Pipitza were both in the kitchen preparing lunch.

"You're exactly the person I wanted to talk to," Silver said.

"Why?" Vula asked.

"I leave for America pretty soon. I wanted to ask what it's like there. What should I expect?"

"I don't know what to say. I have a picture of our house in Houston here in my wallet. I'll show it to you."

Vula took out the picture and handed it to Silver. It was a picture of herself and her groom with their bridesmaids and bridegrooms, in front of the house. A lot of young and healthy looking men and women were gathered on a manicured yard, looking artificially green. The house in the back was constructed of wood. Very different from anything Silver had ever seen.

"It's beautiful." Silver said. "Why did you come here? Wasn't it better to stay there?"

"I don't know. I married George and I came here with him."

"Why did you marry George? Were there not enough men to pick from?"

"There were, I suppose, but he was the man I fell in love with and I wanted to be with him."

"How do you like living here?"

"I like it! I have a small car and drive around Athens. I take care of my baby. I have a good husband. I'm happy!"

"Do you work?"

"I don't have to. Before I had my baby I worked as a secretary at an American company in Athens. Now that I have George to take care of, I stay home."

"How lucky you are." Silver said, and meant it.

Chapter 47

Vuliagmeni

"What are you two talking about?" Maria came from the kitchen through the open doors carrying a tray with coulouretzs and fresh lemonade.

"Silver was asking me about America," Vula answered. "What about going to the beach now, before lunch?" Maria asked.

"I'd like to go." Silver answered.

"I'd rather stay here with George. The sun is not good for him. He has very sensitive skin."

"Silver and I are going for a swim, Maria announced. I'll change into my bathing suit. What about you Silver?"

"I have my bathing suit on, under my clothes. I'm ready to go as soon as you are, Maria."

When Maria come back wearing her full bathing suit and a watertight cap, a towel in her hand, they left for the beaches.

"There is a lake here that has thermal water all year around. Vuliagmeni is well known. The warm water comes from a spring beneath ground. It's a cure for arthritis. People come from all around world to take baths here."

"Let's go to the lake."

The lake was a few blocks away from where they lived. It was in a fenced place with a gated entrance. It had showers and privacy cabins to change in, and had a pool with the therapeutic water for older people to exercise in with long chairs arranged around it on a wooden deck.

The natural spring was to the side coming from a sepulchre forming a small river that had cut its way over time through rocky hills. One could go into the spring and the cavity where the spring came from. The sepulchre was chained so that people who were not good swimmers could not get in there. It was dangerous. There were stories about swimmers trying to go beneath the rocks of the sepulchre to find the origins of the spring and drowning. One could swim in the small river cut between the rocky hills.

Silver swam everywhere, enjoying the warm water and the hidden places among rocks.

Maria went into the pool and exercised along with other people her age.

They changed clothes and returned to the apartment. The table on the veranda was set with a tablecloth and settings for Maria, Pipitza, Vulva and Silver.

Pipitza started to bring out the food she'd prepared. Freshly cooked meatballs, feta cheese, and fresh green salad and pasta with grated Parmesan cheese and freshly cut basil.

A soft, refreshing breeze came from the sea. How tranquil everything was, how peaceful. Some people had it made, but Silver was not one of them!

Chapter 48

Kiki

Silver was seated on the chair next to the refrigerated display window in Vangheli's shop. They discussed her imminent departure. A woman in her thirties, small and wearing tight shorts entered the shop.

"Vangheli. Hi! How are you? Do you remember me? I am Kiki."

"Of course I remember you. It has been a while since I saw you. Are you visiting from America? Where's your husband? Is he with you?"

"No, my husband and children are home. I'm visiting with a tour, with my boss from work. We're going to Egypt to visit the pyramids."

"Whoa, let me look at you! You're still the same." Vangheli said. "How many years has it been?"

"Seventeen. I was only thirteen when I married my husband and left for America."

"I can't believe so many years have passed. You were a child when you worked for me. Now you're a grown woman with a family. How many children do you have?"

"Two girls, sixteen and fourteen."

"I've two children myself, a daughter who's seventeen, and a son who's twenty-two."

"Time flies. I'm here to buy some jewelry. I want to have some bracelets made."

"Kiki, this is my niece, Silver. The daughter of my sister, Thiana, from Romania. She wants to go to the United States. She's looking for somebody to sponsor her in America."

"I could do that. Write your name here for me, and note my name and address too."

"She's going to America through the World Churches Organization. You might have to contact the Organization headquarters there and ask for her by name."

"Write that down too. I'll contact the Organization in America. I live in Florida, in Jacksonville. I'll keep you for ten days at my house until you find yourself a job.

After the ten days you are on your own."

"That's fine." Vangheli said. "She just needs a sponsor to be allowed to leave here to go to America. Once she gets there she'll find her own way."

"O.K. That's set then. I have to go to the jewelry store and see about my bracelets. We leave tomorrow for Egypt. Nice meeting you, Silver. It has been good seeing you, Vangheli."

Kiki left and Silver remained behind to talk to her uncle and inquire about how well he knew Kiki and wondering if she really meant what she said about sponsoring her. Silver personally did not take it seriously. Kiki looked somewhat eccentric with her deep tan and short shorts.

Chapter 49

The American Embassy

At once everything started to move, as if the hand that was spinning the giant time machine had been moving slowly until that time, and had all of a sudden started to move very quickly.

Silver had been in Greece for about eight months and nothing happened with her paperwork until now.

Ms. Nicolau from the World Churches Services called her at Teresa's, and informed her that she was scheduled for the interview at the American Embassy within days. Silver's breathing was labored as she ran down the stairs to Teresa's apartment to talk to Ms. Nicolau on the phone.

"Do you need a translator to accompany you to the interview?" Helene asked.

"Why would I need a translator? I think I can speak English quite well." Silver said.

"Some people request an interpreter even though they speak English very well. I suppose it gives them time to think the answer over."

"Well, I have nothing to hide or think about. I'll speak in English."

"Well, there is a positive side to that, too. The Officer would like to see you speaking English. That might be in your favor. Good luck to you!"

"Thanks, I'll need it." Silver replaced the receiver and turned around to talk to Teresa.

"What do you think?"

"You'll have no problems being accepted. Make sure you don't make the same mistake twice. Do not bring up the problem of your family. That you'll have to solve later, after you are in the United States." Teresa said.

"Yes, I think I learned that lesson the hard way. I'm going upstairs now to start packing. Just in case I'm accepted, I want to be ready to leave at a moment's notice."

Silver went to her garsoniera on the top floor and started to think how best to pack. Her mother had sent her comforter from Romania, and all her winter clothes. There were a lot of things to pack and carry, an entire household she had put together while in Athens. She would have to go to Monostirache at the farmer's market and try to find some navy sacks to pack everything in.

She refused to think about the impending interview. Everybody had told her that it was difficult to be accepted to go to the United States, that a lot of refugees were turned down at the interview. She certainly hoped that would not be the case for her.

She was young and educated and spoke quite fluent English. She wouldn't bring up the problem with her family again. She wouldn't mention that her most cherished desire was to bring her family out of Romania, to be reunited with them wherever she would land, hopefully to the United States.

On the day of the interview, she dressed carefully, to look clean and professional and composed. She went to the American Embassy and waited to be called for the interview. She was waiting on the second floor of a large mansion. Silver looked around curiously. The house looked more like an elegant villa than an embassy, with its hard wood floors and tall sunny windows. French doors covered with drapes led to the interviewing room. Finally a big burly man in his thirties came out and invited her inside his office. The room was large and airy. The tall windows were open and the white curtains billowed in the breeze. Behind the mahogany desk was a fireplace and just to the right was the American flag with its golden eagle tip.

"For the record, please state your full name and your address. I have to let you know that the interview is taped."

"I'm Silver Costin and I live at 39 Nikifor Uranou, here in Athens.

"What is your country of birth?"

"I was born in Greece and raised in Romania."

"Are you a Greek or a Romanian citizen then?"

"I'm a Romanian citizen, like my father."

"Why are you here?"

"I applied to emigrate to the United States of America."

"I see from your application here that you are an engineer."

"Yes."

"What kind of an Engineer?"

"I'm a Civil Engineer. I graduated from the Faculty of Hydrotechnical Constructions in Bucharest."

"So, do you plan to seek employment in the United States?"

"That's right. As soon as I get there."

"Well, you know that we Americans are spoiled. Some Americans choose not to work."

"And how are they supporting themselves if they're not working?" Silver asked totally taken aback.

"They rely on the government to pay their way "

"How that come?"

"The Government has a Social Security program which allows for a minimal living arrangements."

"I'm planning to work. And very hard. I studied for a long time in college and I want to apply what I know. I love my engineering job."

"And why is that?"

"I love the creativity of it. You come up with an idea in your head and make it work on the ground."

"Americans are so spoiled. People are taking their liberties for granted in America. They even elect not to go to vote. Did you had a chance to vote in your county?"

"Yes of course, after I was 18 years of age. But the voting was automatic. The names were already on the ballot. The only thing we had to do was fold it and slip it in the box."

"You'll get the freedom in America to choose whom you think is a better representative for you. Now tell me the truth. Why do you want to leave your country? For economic reasons? Do you hope for a better life in America? You know, we don't allow immigrants into America just because they desire a better lifestyle."

"That too. I'd like a better lifestyle. But that was not my primary reason for defecting from my country. We had jobs and salaries, and my parents had owned the house before the war. I don't think we were considered to be poor."

"Then why? You know it's not going to be easy in America, at least in the beginning."

"Well, they were putting pressure on me at work to became a party member. In the Communist Party."

"And you did not want to do so?"

"Well, if I had accepted, later on they could have forced me to do things I wouldn't have agreed with doing."

"Like what?"

"I don't know. But I cannot compromise. I'm the kind of person who does only what my conscience dictates."

"I see. Do you know what is here behind me?"

"I think I do. It's the American flag."

"You'll have to swear by the American Flag when you became an American citizen. You'll have to renounce your Romanian citizenship. Are you going to do so?"

"I'll be proud to do so."

"By the way, congratulations on your English. It's quite good."

"Thank you. I have been studding very hard since I arrived here."

"How long have you been here in Athens?"

"It's been eight months now."

"Your application is dated recently. What did you do for eight months here?"

"Well, my mother is Greek and she has relatives here. It was her wish that I stay here in Greece."

"Then what happened?"

"I tried. I even went before the "Epitropi" of the Greek government."

"And?"

"They might had approved me to stay here, but they were unwilling to help me bring my family over from Romania."

"You know those are small countries. They don't want to get in the middle of a sticky problem with their neighboring Romania over your family."

"I understand."

"Well, the United States will help you bring your family over there. Once you're an American citizen you can apply for your family to be reunited with you in the United States. That's the law."

"It that true?" Silver could not believe her ears. "That's my most cherished desired, of course. To be reunited with my family."

"You'll be able to do so in the United States."

What a relief to know that from the beginning. She had to call her mother right away to tell her the good news.

Before she knew, everything was over.

"Piece of cake." Silver thought, breezing through the door to the sunshine outside. The big man, the Officer, even joked about the fact that she wasn't married yet and she'd need to do so. He seemed quite friendly. Silver had a good feeling about the interview.

Within a few days Ms. Nicolau from the World Churches Services called her back and told her that indeed she'd been accepted. The next step would be the physical examination. She had no problems with that. She was in perfect health.

The only remaining thing was to find a "sponsor" for her in the United States. She hoped that her uncle from New York, or maybe Kiki, the lady from Jacksonville, had contacted the World Churches Services to sponsor her. Meanwhile she had to finish packing, in order to be ready to leave whenever they would let her know and gave her the air plane ticket.

There was one problem, unresolved, nagging constantly at the back of her mind. It was tagging at the strings of her heart, weakening her resolution to go to America, eroding her energy. Costas. She had told him about her impending departure and his reaction seamed indifferent. She did not know what to make out of it. She'd pressed the issue by asking Maria to be more direct on her behalf. No answer. Short of asking him to marry her, she had done everything she knew how to do. She had no time for idle thoughts now. She had to move ahead with her plans for America. And this time the rapid sequence of events pushed her toward that direction.

Chapter 50

Costas

"Hi! It's me. I just hung up with my mother back in Romania. They're very exited about me being approved to go to America."

"I thought so! Who wouldn't like to go to America."

"Well, I told them they'll be able to join me there in five years after I became an American citizen." "Who told you so?"

"They told me at the American Embassy at the interview, and also I confirmed it with Ms. Nicolau at the World Council of Churches. I have the right to ask for my immediate family after I become an American citizen. That means my parents, brother, and sister. Of course if I were to me married, I could ask for my husband right away within the first two years after my arrival." She thought she'd throw that in, just in case he'd be interested.

"It's that so."

"Yes."

"Well you know that I studied in England for five years. I got my master's degree in engineering. And that I am not very happy here with my work and everything. Who knows, I might decide to join you in America soon."

"That'd be wonderful, indeed." Silver could not believe her ears. He had finally spoken his mind.

"Well, we'll see."

Silver hung up the phone and started dreaming with her eyes wide open. Did it mean Costas was considering marring her? Coming to find her in America? That would be the ultimate dream. He was an engineer too. A safety engineer with fluent English, he would be able to land a job. Maybe even before her. He was a man after all. And it was still a man's world.

Chapter 51

Raffia

Mimis invited Silver to spend the weekend at his house in Raffia. Silver prepared to go. She wore her yellow skirt and white halter top, and packed enough clothes for changes including of course, her bathing suit. Mimis told her his house was right on the beach. She was looking forward to it.

At noon on Saturday, she took the bus to Raffia from Platia Panipestimiou. The bus fare was relatively cheap. For 45 lepta one could travel as far as Sonyo on the coast and as far as Raffia.

It took about two hours to get there. When she got off the bus, she followed the directions Mimis had given her the day before. She arrived at the given address. It was a new, tall, multi-level building located right on the beach. There were people already gathered there.

Mimis took her on a tour of the building, pointing out his apartment on the first floor. Next door to his apartment was the apartment of his girlfriend. She and her husband and daughter owned the apartment, and spent weekends and summer vacations there.

Mimis pointed out a garsoniera next to it on the same floor and referred to it as Costas' apartment. Silver did not ask any more questions because Costas had not mentioned to her that he had an apartment in Mimis' building on the beach, at Raffia. Maybe Mimis was referring to another Costas. Silver didn't want to appear nosy by asking too many questions.

Mimis' wife, who didn't look so ugly after all, invited her to unpack her clothes in the guest bedroom of their apartment. The apartment was furnished with antique furniture, heavy mahogany pieces, intricately carved.

As far as Silver could tell they were preparing for a party that evening. Mimi's wife told her that they prepared a "Proxenia". This was the first meeting of a young man and woman with matrimonial intentions. The parents of the young girl or her relatives prearranged the date. In this case the young girl was a relative of Mimis' girlfriend, and she was giving the party.

Silver didn't pay much attention to the preparations because she hardly knew Mimis' girlfriend or his wife, and she sensed the tension between the two rival women as they were preparing and arranging the food. It was not her business to ask question or interfere. She was there for a fun, relaxing weekend. If that included a party and two people meeting with marriage in their minds, it certainly was not her business to interfere.

Chapter 52

Raffia

They returned to the house.

"Here you are. I would like you to meet my mother." Mimis said, turning towards the old lady that accompanied him.

"Glad to meet you, Silver. Pipitza has told me so much about you. I'm glad to finally have met you."

"I've heard a lot about you too." Silver took the arm of the old lady.

"Would you like to go for a walk around the neighborhood?" Mimis' mother asked.

"Yes, of course. I'd like to see the surroundings."

They went for a stroll around the neighborhood. It was a small village, Silver thought, as they passed through its narrow dirt roads lined with small houses. Only Mimis' policatekia raised proudly above the neighboring houses and above the sea.

"Do you know Costas?" Silver asked the old lady.

"Of course I know Costas. He's a very good friend of Mimis."

"I'm dating him and I really like him a lot." Silver felt instinctively that she could trust the older woman with her confession.

"Is that so." The old lady seemed interested. "Then Mimis shouldn't have invited you today."

"Why not? I'm glad to have met you and his wife and daughter and see what a grand mansion he has."

The old lady didn't comment, and they returned slowly to the house. By now a lot of other guests had gathered.

The young girl who was to be presented at the proxenia was now at the house, and both Mimis' wife and his girlfriend were fussing around her to dress her up and arrange her hair in the most becoming manner. The groom had to like her.

Silver stayed away from it all. They were foreign customs to her. She simply enjoyed the beauty of her natural surroundings, and the sea breeze. It was getting dark.

Chapter 53

The show down

The table was nicely arranged on the veranda, the wide balcony wrapping around the entire first floor of the building. The guests were talking and laughing amongst themselves. The nifi-bride was beautifully arrayed, her dress becoming, her hair arranged to perfection. She was a young girl of maybe eighteen or nineteen years, Silver thought, and she was slender and tall.

Pretty, Silver thought, without paying a second thought to the girl. She had her own problems to think of, and what Mimis' mother and the man she went swimming with had told her about Costas were at the front of her mind.

She had to figure out a way to make Costas love her, if he didn't love her by now! She missed him so much.

Nobody paid any attention to Silver as she sat by herself next to the balustrade. She hadn't taken the time to arrange herself after the swimming. She wore her skirt and halter-top directly over her wet bathing suit. Her hair was disheveled and she didn't pay any attention to her looks. It was getting close to eleven o'clock and the groom hadn't appeared yet. Everybody waited for him, along with the <u>nifi</u>.

Finally, at eleven o'clock, Costas appeared. Silver couldn't believe her eyes. It was Costas, her Costas, dressed up elegantly for the evening with his black waved hair combed back. He was wearing a wide silk tie at his neck.

Silver froze in place, looking at him, her mouth wide open. It couldn't be. He couldn't possibly be the groom. What a nightmare. Costas said good evening to everybody from the stairway. He passed by Silver without even glancing toward her. He said an inaudible "Hello, there." as he passed, without even moving his lips. He walked by and sat at the table next to the nifi-bride.

Everybody started talking at once and patting him on the shoulder, joking loudly about him and the girl. Silver was forgotten in the dark, by the railing, alone. She started trembling. Mimis' wife noticed her and offered to bring her a sweater, thinking she was cold. Mimis' wife brought her a black, thick sweater that Silver shrugged into.

Silver heard that they were preparing to go to a discotheque to dance. Mimis came to her and invited her to go along. Silver's brain was dead. She couldn't think, she couldn't feel anything, she was numb with pain.

She felt like staying right there in her damp clothes, by herself. She did not want to go anywhere. What for? To watch Costas and the <u>nifi</u> dancing together and having fun? The hurt inside her heart was numbing. She would have liked to crawl down on the floor and lie there crying all by herself. No way of doing that in the middle of all those people.

So everything was a lie? Why was Costas going out with her? What did he want from her if he had his mind set on marrying somebody else? Did he think she was an easy mark, because she was alone and vulnerable? He did not love her. Was it just lust from his side? He and Mimis were best friends, after all. Perhaps they were making fun of her behind her back? Maybe the men at the office had been trying to warn her that Costas was a double timer by saying bad things about him in front of her? And she had thought that Costas loved her and would follow her to America. What a fool she had been! And the whole time he had been dating her, Costas had been making plans to marry somebody else. Of course, a girl with "prika". If the girl was related to Mimis' girlfriend she was probably rich. In all fairness, the girl was young and pretty. She had none of Silver's problems with the immigration, with the family left behind in Romania whom she had to rescue. Why not marry the young girl? It was so much simpler. But why didn't Costas say something to her beforehand? Why did Mimis invite her there? To see for herself? To hurt her? Why? Did Costas know she was invited too? Did he care at all? They wanted to crush her. To crush her pride, to humiliate her, to dismantle her of her human dignity, the only thing she had left. Why did they hate her so? She had done no harm to any of them. Evil took different faces, she thought bitterly. Ugly faces like Mimis', or pretty faces like Costas'. She'd not let them see how deeply they had hurt her. She would not give them the satisfaction of watching her crumble with pain right there, in front of their eyes. She'd find a way out.

Finally she changed her clothes, and went along with the crowd. She was seated on a chair next to the wall, facing Costas and the bride who were seated next to each other in the middle of the room. She'd get violently sick in a matter of minutes if she stayed there. How could she escape? The busses didn't circulate at that hour of the night. Or on the next day, Sunday. She had to figure out a way to escape from there, and quickly. Before she got sick and let these people know how terribly, how mortally, they had wounded her.

She looked over and noticed a fat man sitting by himself. She remembered she had seen him arriving by himself, later that evening. She'd ask him to drive her to Athens, now. She might have to pretend that she liked him to get him to drive her home. She went over to sit next to the fat man and in a cheery voice asked him to drive her to Athens. He agreed. Silver and the fat man disappeared in the night. Silver went and picked up her light bag from Mimis' apartment and left without saying a word to anybody.

Chapter 54

Vuliagmeni

Through her numbness, Silver could hear the fat man seated next to her in the red Porsche talking about his wife leaving him and running away with another man. It was around three o'clock in the morning before Silver got home. The fat man proved to be a gentleman and drove her to her apartment without incident. He was happy to have somebody to listen to his story.

Silver went to bed, and could not sleep. At sunrise the next morning, she woke up, dressed as if in a trance, took her overnight bag already packed from the night before and left for Vuliagmeni, to Maria's. The busses started to run around six o'clock in the morning. She would be there by eight o'clock, when everybody was awake, she thought.

When she arrived at the apartment that Maria and Pipitza rented for the summer at Vuliagmeni, Silver made it to the doorway and rang the bell. After that she couldn't remember what happened to her.

When she awoke, she was in a bed next to Evghenia's bed. She had a terrible headache, her eyes pulsated and throbbed with pain, and she was nauseated. Pipitza came with a pot and cold wet towels, cooling her forehead and holding her head while she threw up. Maria appeared in the doorway with a glass of water and aspirin.

They both cursed Mimis for his cruelty. Probably, Silver thought, she'd had enough energy and told them what happened before she had passed out.

Everything would be fine now, Silver thought. She was among friends. Caring, loving hands were attending to her. She could go to sleep now. Everything was going to be O.K., Silver thought, as she drifted to sleep.

She woke up in the afternoon and first thing she noticed was Evghenia laying in the bed next to her with her foot raised up on a pillow, all in white gypsum.

"How you're doing, Evghenia?"

"Ooh! As good as I could be with my foot all in pieces and a pin in my ankle. That stupid husband of mine! He was probably on medication when he ran the car into a pole. I'm going to leave him as soon as I can walk."

"What happened exactly?"

"He was driving and probably fell asleep, because the next thing I know we were against a pole and my foot was all messed up. It took them four hours in the emergency room to set up my ankle. They do not know for sure if I'll be able to walk without a limp. And he escaped without even a scratch. The car, my car, is a pile of rubble now!"

"Do you really think he was on medication?"

"I know that for a fact. He has mental problems! I'm going to divorce him as soon as I'm on my feet!"

"Did you know before you married him that he had health problems?"

"No, of course not! He hid it well. I thought I married somebody, a lawyer, and in fact he was really ill."

"Do you love him or did you love him when you married him?"

"No, I had to get married! But if he had loved me, I would have looked like a doll, not so fat as I am now. He doesn't love me. He makes me unhappy. That's why I eat so much. He needed somebody to take care of him, that's why he married me."

Somehow Silver doubted Evghenia was fat because her husband didn't love her. Actually she doubted that if he really loved her, Evghenia would be slim. She liked to eat too much.

"Mimis' mother called." Evghenia added. "She apologized for Mimis inviting you there. He claimed he didn't know that you loved Costas and were dating him. What a snake Mimis is! Like all men! Probably he would have liked you for himself, but he was married and couldn't do anything inappropriate with Mother being friends with his mother."

Chapter 55

The End

Silver stayed at Vuliagmeni all weekend. On Monday she returned home, and started to think seriously about packing her belongings and preparing for the imminent journey to America. The wound inside her heart was still open, but she decided to move forward and think positively about the future without dwelling on the past. She'd have all her life to do that. Dwell on the past. Now she had to concentrate on moving forward. Her life and her family's life depended on her. No time for mourning right now. She'd have to do that later.

* * *

Her vacation to Greece had come to an end. It had lasted one year and two months. It was the most beautiful time in her life, despite all of the problems she had encountered. It was a time for her to grow into an independent woman.

It was the only time when she did not have to work, to have a scheduled life, an eight to five office job. It was the only time in her life when she was by herself. It was the only time in her life when she felt free, totally free like a butterfly in the sunshine.

And just as the butterfly is fascinated by the light, she went too close to the heat source, burning her delicate wings over and over again.

-The end-

Chapter 56

Epilogue 1

It was her last night in Greece.

All her belongings were neatly packed in big navy sacks, neatly sewn.

She had visited all her relatives and her friends and acquaintances, and said her goodbyes.

She ordered a taxi for the next morning to take her to the airport. She was ready to go.

But on this last night, Athens and Greece were still hers.

Silver went on the terrace, outside her <u>garsoniera</u>. The terrace encompassed the entire building's roof. She, or rather the man who rented the top floor garsoniera before her, had a wrought iron table and a chair just outside the door on the terrace.

Silver went outside and sat on the chair.

The night was clear, stars shining and the moon showing clear and close, as if she could touch them if she stretched out her hand.

In the building across the street from her, a window on the second floor was lit. A young woman dressed in a halter-top prepared dinner. No curtains obstructed the view.

High on the Licavitos, the little white church Aghios Dimitrios was illuminated as if in daylight.

Silver felt her heart full, ready to burst, tears stinging her eyes.

The air in Athens was sweet smelling, like an aphrodisiac. It was the feeling of love, or better yet the imminent prospect of it, in the air.

That night Athens and Greece were hers to drink in, to satiate her soul.

Tomorrow, another chapter of her life would start.

Chapter 57

Epilogue 2

It was her last night in Greece.

All her belongings were neatly packed in big navy sacks, neatly sewn.

She visited all her relatives and her friends and acquaintances, here in Greece, and said her goodbye.

She ordered a taxi for the next morning to take her to the airport. She was ready to go.

But this last night, Athens and Greece were still hers.

Silver went on the terrace, outside her garsoniera.

The terrace encompassed the entire building's roof. She, or better said the man who rented the top floor garsoniera before her, had a glass and wrought iron table and a chair, just outside the door on the terrace.

Silver went outside and sat on the chair.

The night was clear, stars shining and the moon showing clear, close, as if she could touch them, if she stretched out her hand.

In the building across the street from her, a window on the second floor was lighted. A young woman dressed in a halter-top prepared dinner. No curtains obstructed the view.

High on the Licavitos the little white Church, Aghios Dimitrios, was lighted as if it were day light.

Silver felt her heart full, ready to burst, tears stinging her eyes.

The air in Athens was sweet smelling, aphrodisiac. It was the feeling of love, or better yet the imminent prospect of it, in the air.

That night, Athens and Greece were hers to drink in, to satiate her soul.

Tomorrow, another chapter of her life would start.

CPSIA information can be obtained
at www.ICGtesting.com
Printed in the USA
BVHW051114130723
667186BV00015B/1256